Aida Matthews

DESKTOP DEVOTIONS
FOR WORKING WOMEN

DESKTOP DEVOTIONS
for
WORKING WOMEN

ELSA HOUTZ

NAVPRESS

A MINISTRY OF THE NAVIGATORS
P.O. BOX 6000, COLORADO SPRINGS, COLORADO 80934

The Navigators is an international Christian organization. Jesus Christ gave His followers the Great Commission to go and make disciples (Matthew 28:19). The aim of The Navigators is to help fulfill that commission by multiplying laborers for Christ in every nation.

NavPress is the publishing ministry of The Navigators. NavPress publications are tools to help Christians grow. Although publications alone cannot make disciples or change lives, they can help believers learn biblical discipleship, and apply what they learn to their lives and ministries.

© 1991 by Elsa M. Houtz

Library of Congress Catalog Card Number: 91-61426
ISBN 08910-96310

Printed in the United States of America

CONTENTS

Introduction: Whoa, There!

PART ONE: ORIENTATION
1. Heaven Sent
2. Taking Root
3. Here's Your Change
4. I'm in Charge Here—I Think
5. What's a Woman to Do?
6. Oops! I Forgot!

PART TWO: TOOLS OF THE TRADE
7. What Every Working Woman Needs
8. Using the Round File
9. Call Out the Guards!
10. Beautiful You
11. 101 Ways to Use a Gift

12. The Eye of the Beholder
13. Where's the Rest?
14. A Blast from the Past
15. My Lord, What a Morning!
16. Good Night
17. It's About Time

PART THREE: ON-THE-JOB
 TRAINING
18. Playing by the Rules
19. Comparison Shopping
20. Ol' Green Eyes
21. I Just Want My Share
22. A Troublemaker? *Moi?*
23. Am I Cracking Up?
24. Cross My Heart
25. Staying in Shape
26. The Dog Ate My Homework
27. Eyeball to Eyeball

PART FOUR: EMPLOYEE BENEFITS
28. A Little Seasoning
29. What a Difference!
30. This Year's Newest Model
31. If You Please
32. Work, Work, Work

To the glory of God
and
to Traci, with thanks.

AUTHOR

Elsa Houtz has been among the ranks of America's working women for over twenty years, in jobs ranging from waitress to college instructor. A former radio newscaster, magazine editor, and advertising copywriter, she is currently the public relations manager for a health care agency. She is a veteran Sunday school teacher and is active in her church.

Elsa lives with her husband and teenage son in Saint Petersburg, Florida.

INTRODUCTION: WHOA, THERE!

In the last place I worked, all the offices in my department opened onto one long hallway that connected us to the rest of the building. Anytime I left my office, no matter where I was headed, I had to use the hallway to get there.

I always moved pretty fast in those days. My high-pressure job involved juggling numerous personalities and projects, and I was constantly driven by self-imposed pressure to complete the most work possible in the least amount of time. I confess: I was a classic corporate superwoman.

One day, in my usual fast-forward mode, I jumped up from my desk and went flying out into the hallway, intent on completing one more task before my next meeting. I raced out into the hallway, full speed ahead — but then I had to stop abruptly right outside my own door because suddenly, I couldn't remember what I was in such a big hurry to do! I looked around blankly, searching for some clue as to where I had been headed, but I couldn't remember. I had left my desk with a specific intention, but by the time I got into the hallway, my mind had raced ahead to something else and had left my original intention lost in obscurity. I slowly went back into my office, sat down at my desk, and laughed.

After a moment it occurred to me that the picture of myself standing helplessly in the hallway, full of frantic energy but with no real destination, seemed to symbolize my hectic life. I knew I had something important to learn from that moment. It was time to slow down.

This book is designed to help us as working women to slow down, take a minute to catch our breath, and, above all, reestablish for ourselves where we're headed. In our full, busy lives, it's easy to feel pushed and pulled and yanked and pressured to do and go and be and fulfill and nurture and create and accomplish. As a result, we lose sight of where we're going and what we really want our lives to be like. Finishing the day's filing becomes more important than listening patiently to a friend who's hurting. Impressing the boss with that month-end report takes priority over demonstrating Christlike patience when the pressure is on. Earning that year-end bonus for increased productivity starts to take precedence over fulfilling commitments to family, friends, and church. Suddenly we are racing headlong toward a destination we never wanted, and we find ourselves becoming someone we don't want to be instead of the women of God we truly desire to be.

God calls us to lives of serenity and inner peace, yet most of the time we let those qualities of life be taken from us. We let the demands of work, home, family, relationships, and church and community activities become burdensome instead of satisfying. Because of the way we deal with these responsibilities, they cause us pressure instead of pleasure.

Each chapter in *Desktop Devotions for Working Women* starts with the challenge "Let's slow down today to. . . ." My hope is that taking a few moments throughout the workday to reflect on this challenge will help each of us refocus our thoughts and reorient our days. The ultimate goal of this book is to help working women reclaim the joy, the richness, and the serenity that God offers us. We can do that only if we are willing to slow down and listen for His voice.

You can use this devotional book in a number of ways. You may want to write or type the Scripture verses at the beginning of each chapter onto note cards or pieces of paper and use them as Scripture memory aids. Then tape them to your mirror at home or post them at your work station, where you can review the verse throughout the day.

The challenges at the beginning of each chapter can be used the same way. Let them stimulate your thinking about that particular topic and help you set goals for your spiritual growth.

Since the book has thirty-two chapters, you can easily use it as a daily devotional for a month. After you've read all the chapters, you may want to go back and review the Scripture verses or read each set of challenges again and see how you've progressed toward those goals.

Translating God's principles and promises into the nitty-gritty of our daily living is one of the most exciting tasks along the route of our walk with Him: doing that is what this book is about. As you journey through these pages, may you find insight, encouragement, and enjoyment. May you experience daily a greater awareness of God's work in your life—and of His work in *your* work.

PART ONE

ORIENTATION

ONE

Heaven Sent

Then I heard the voice of the Lord saying,
"Whom shall I send? And who will go for us?"
And I said, "Here am I.
Send me!"

Isaiah 6:8

I t's 4:00 Friday afternoon. You're busy working at your desk when your boss, Sandy, comes out of her office and announces to you and your coworkers:

"The main office just called. They have to have the month-end reports by 5:00, which means someone has to take them over there in the next few minutes. I've got a board meeting in half an hour so I can't do it. I know this involves a trip across town at rush hour, but it has to be done. Lucy, would you go for me?"

"Gee, Sandy, I'd like to help you out," Lucy says, "but I've got to pick up my son at baseball practice at 4:30. I was just getting ready to leave. Could you ask someone else?"

Sandy looks at Dan, who's busily rummaging in his desk drawer and trying to become invisible.

"Dan, how about it?" she asks.

"I'd be glad to—but I can't. I promised some guys I'd meet them at the gym to play basketball after work. If I don't go, they won't have enough players for their team. See if you can get someone else, okay?"

"Well, Jean, how about you?" Sandy says to your other coworker. "I guess you'll need to do it."

"Sure, Sandy," Jean says, "just as long as I get overtime and mileage."

Since you were the only one left, you breathe a sigh of relief and a word of thanks that Jean at least agreed to make the trip. With work to finish, groceries to buy, kids to pick up from the sitter's, supper to fix, and a ball game to make by 7:00 p.m., the last thing you needed was to make an extra trip across town!

■

Most people don't like to be sent to do things. One of the traditional rules of the workplace, like the military, is "Never volunteer." When the boss is looking for someone to send on an errand or work on a special project, most of us are more likely to respond "Sorry, I can't" than "I'll do it. Send me."

Why?

Maybe, like Lucy, we have other responsibilities that we feel are more important. Or maybe we're like Dan, and we don't want anything to interfere with our recreation or social life. Sometimes we're probably like Jean; we don't want to go out of our way unless there's something in it for us.

Apparently no one told the prophet Isaiah that volunteering was dangerous. When God asked who would prophesy to His people for Him, Isaiah didn't have the good sense to make himself scarce. Instead, we can almost picture him stepping right up, waving his hand high in the air, and saying in a loud voice, "Here I am, Lord. I'll do it. How about sending me?" He was more than willing to be sent to do God's work.

So was Jesus. "I have come down from heaven," He said, "not to do my will but to do the will of him who sent me" (John 6:38).

Those of us who are Christians in the workplace have been sent by God to do His work there: to reflect His qualities of patience, kindness, goodness, integrity, and compassion; to demonstrate unconditional love and acceptance; to tell others that life can be rich and satisfying and joyful even in the face of adversity; to encourage, to care, to reach out; to stand firmly for what is right, regardless of what is profitable or expedient. In short, as His ambassadors to the working world, we have been sent to draw others to Him and to live by Christ's example.

Of course, we don't *have* to say "Send me!" when God calls for women to take His message to the workplace. We can just tell Him we're too busy. Or too tired. Or we can tell Him there's not enough in it for us. We can coast along, looking and acting and living like everyone else. We can go along with the crowd, whether their attitudes and behavior are compatible with our Christian beliefs or not. We can do that. After all, God won't reach down and pluck us from the earth if we do.

We can even try the prophet Jeremiah's "but-I'm-not-good-enough" excuse. When God called him to prophesy to His people, Jeremiah said, "I do not know how to speak; I am only a child" (Jeremiah 1:6). Moses tried this approach, too. When God called him to lead the Hebrews out of Egypt, he said, "O Lord, I have never been eloquent. . . . Please send someone else to do it" (Exodus 4:10,13).

From Jeremiah and from Moses and from us, God doesn't ask for perfection; He only asks for willingness. But, since we have the gift of free will, we can choose not to be willing. Basking comfortably in our own shortcomings, we can convince ourselves we're just not the woman for the job He has in mind.

Yes, we can let someone else do it. After all, there are plenty of other Christians around, aren't there? We, like Moses, can ask God to send someone else.

We can do that. We can turn our backs when God says, "Whom can I send? Who will go?"

But if we do, we will miss out on the glorious mission He has for us: bringing Jesus Christ to a confused, hurting, and lonely world.

PRAYER

Father, I know You need women to bring Your good news into the workplace. Please send me. I'm not perfect (as You know), but I'll try, Lord. Open my heart to Your Spirit to be my teacher and guide. Let me be the one to help my coworkers see the glorious life You hold out for them. Here I am, Lord. Send me. Amen.

T W O

Taking Root

*Blessed is the man who trusts in the LORD. . . .
He will be like a tree planted by the water that
sends out its roots by the stream. It does not
fear when heat comes; its leaves are always
green. It has no worries in a year of drought
and never fails to bear fruit.*

Jeremiah 17:7-8

A t first glance, it looked like just another baby tree, just another one of the millions of Ponderosa pines that make up the Pike National Forest in the Colorado Rockies. It was barely three feet tall. Its puny trunk wasn't more than an inch in diameter. But it was arrow-straight. And the tree's skinny little branches sprouted fat clusters of lush, long needles with the green freshness that only young trees have.

Amazingly, this tree had sprouted out of what looked like a tablespoonful of dirt wedged in a narrow crack in a granite boulder the size of a tractor tire. The boulder sat atop a rocky ridge, nearly 8,000 feet above sea level. On the day I was there, the wind was blowing ferociously—so hard that I couldn't stand up on the rocks around the tree. In fact, I had to sit down to avoid being blown over. The wind whipped the little tree mercilessly too, sometimes forcing it almost flat against the rock. But each time the wind subsided, the tree stood erect again, undaunted.

In the moments between the wind's powerful gusts, the sun's heat was blistering; I could feel it baking the top of my head and the skin on my face. Like the wind, though, the sun's heat left the little tree unscathed. Its bright needles showed no signs of wilting or drying out. This skinny, impudent little pine tree seemed to be daring the wind and the sun to do their worst, utterly confident that its roots would hold it firm—no matter what.

For a long time, I couldn't stop looking at the tree, couldn't stop thinking about its ability to withstand the powerful forces around it. I knew it had something to tell you and me about our lives as Christian women in the working world.

Like the tree, we are faced with powerful forces in our environment. As Christian women in the workplace, we face hostile forces that work to uproot us from our moorings in Christ: pressure to conform to the world's standards; temptation to be influenced by others' opinions and behavior even when we know they're wrong; desire to pursue the world's treasures instead of God's riches; the expedience of cultivating conditional, self-seeking relationships instead of unconditional love.

The Bible challenges us repeatedly with the concept of *rootedness*, that is, of remaining firmly anchored amid the world's forces. The apostle Paul spoke of the Christian believers at Ephesus as "being rooted and established in love" (Ephesians 3:17). Like the prophet Jeremiah in the passage at the beginning of today's devotion, the psalmist also compared a godly person to "a tree planted by streams of water, which yields its fruit in season and whose leaf does not wither" (Psalm 1:3). Even Jesus talked about rootedness. He told of those who "receive the word with joy when they hear it, but they have no root. They believe for a while, but in the time of testing they fall away" (Luke 8:13).

We cannot bring Christ's example and message into the workplace on our own strength alone. Our love is inadequate to override the conflicts and tensions that can arise in on-the-job relationships. Our patience is inadequate to endure day-to-day frustrations with grace. Our compassion is too limited to give priority to the needs of others when we're short on time and low on energy.

Our resistance to temptation is too weak to withstand the working world's promise that more money and more power will bring us happiness. Unless we are firmly rooted in Him, we dry out and blow away, leaving an empty place where we once took a stand for Christ.

So, how can we strengthen our roots?

■ By coming to work each day armed with God's Word in our hearts, which means starting each workday with time for Bible reading.

■ By cultivating the consciousness of God's presence throughout our workday.

■ By challenging ourselves to confront problems that arise on the job by asking the very simple question "What would Jesus do?"

■ By making a practice of looking at others through Christ's eyes, so that we see their unique gifts and deepest needs rather than their shortcomings.

We are called to strengthen our spiritual roots: "Just as you received Christ Jesus as Lord, continue to live in him, rooted and built up in him, strengthened in the faith as you were taught, and overflowing with thankfulness" (Colossians 2:6-7). How can *you* strengthen your spiritual roots and build yourself up in Him as you go about your daily life?

PRAYER

God, help me to remain firmly rooted in You. I'm so susceptible to the world's wind and sun — taking the easy route instead of the right one; letting negative thoughts and unkind words take the place of Christlike ones; being swayed by the pressure of what others think and do so I won't be an oddball. If a tiny pine tree can stand against the blistering sun and ferocious wind, surely with Your help I can take a stand for You in my place of work. Amen.

THREE

Here's Your Change

Then he [Jesus] said to his disciples, "The harvest is plentiful but the workers are few. Ask the Lord of the harvest, therefore, to send out workers into his harvest field."

Matthew 9:37-38

LET'S SLOW DOWN TODAY TO...

≈ *consider how we can make a difference in the world;*

≈ *practice seeing ourselves as Christ's agents for change.*

Joan is a first-grade teacher. She's been selected as one of a very few teachers in her school district to participate in an experimental teaching program during the coming school year. Through this program, Joan and others like her help children who do poorly in school by giving them a great deal of individual attention and one-to-one teaching. In other school districts that have tried such methods, the programs have been very successful in helping students improve.

Joan is excited about being a part of the project.

"I just feel like maybe this program will give me a chance to make a real difference in these children's lives," she says. "So often, I feel like I work in my classroom day after day but don't really change anything for these students. They either get held back to repeat first grade, or they go into second grade and do poorly there. Maybe through this program I can actually help change the pattern of failure for them."

Joan is like many Christian women who enter fields like teaching, medicine, social work, and various forms of Christian ministry. We want, above all, to make a difference. We see the suffering and despair and social ills around us, and we want to help change things.

Christians are called to make a difference, to change things, to bring good into an evil and hurting world. Sometimes, like Joan, we feel as if the odds are overwhelming; the forces of evil and despair are too powerful for us; our puny efforts just tire us out and don't really change anything. The Bible encourages us not to give up, though. "Let us not become weary in doing good," Paul told the Galatian church, "for at the proper time we will reap a harvest if we do not give up" (Galatians 6:9).

The opportunity to make a difference isn't limited to occupations like teaching or ministry. Can you think of the individuals in your life who have had a strong, positive effect on you? Your parents? A friend who was there when you thought your life was falling apart? A coworker whose caring and gentle spirit brightened your workdays? A boss who genuinely cared about helping you make the most of your job?

Making a difference doesn't have to mean changing the course of a person's life; it can mean simply changing the quality of a day, or even a moment. What about the grocery cashier who always gives you a cheerful greeting when you rush in at the end of a long, tiring workday? The friend who's always ready to share both your joys and disappointments? The supervisor who says, "You're doing a great job" just when you think the overtime is going to kill you? The Christian friend who helps you put day-to-day problems into a biblical perspective?

Jesus made a difference in every life He touched. We can, too, if we make that our goal.

Where are the opportunities in your life to bring about change? Look around you—in your workplace, your neighborhood, your church, your club. There is more than enough pain, uncertainty, hopelessness, confusion, anger, and hatred all around us. We don't have to look far to find countless opportunities to bring about positive change.

Being an agent for change may mean demonstrating Christ's love and acceptance to a person who feels unloved and unlovable. It may mean helping someone find a job after a layoff, or baking a casserole for a family in which a member is ill or injured. It may mean sympathizing with a friend who's had a death in her family and reassuring her of God's promise of eternal life. It may mean showing patience to a difficult child or angry coworker, or being willing to let others take the credit for *your* job well done. Or it may mean starting a program to find homes and jobs for homeless families.

Being an agent for change can mean changing the quality of one moment, or changing the course of history. We can help change the way people think and feel about themselves, or about others, or about the future, or about what is truly important in their lives.

We can be Christ's agents for change without burning ourselves out by trying to do more than is realistic or even possible for us. We are each equipped differently to bring about change, and God calls each of us to different tasks. Our challenge is to be diligent and faithful and to rely on God's guidance as we work to reap a harvest for Him.

PRAYER

God, I am excited to think that You can use me to bring about change in the world. Help me to use the unique gifts, circumstances, and resources You have given me to make a difference in the lives of others — today, and every day. Amen.

FOUR

I'm in Charge Here- I Think

What is man that you are mindful of him, the son of man that you care for him? . . . You made him ruler over the works of your hands; you put everything under his feet.

Psalm 8:4,6

What do the things in this list have in common?

Clock	Commercials
Computer	Car pool
Calendar	Cleaning
Company	Calories

If you're saying they all begin with the letter C, you're right, of course; but in this case that isn't the answer. What these things have in common is that, in one way or another, they all seem to *control* us from time to time.

For example, the clock dictates how much time we have to do things, how soon we have to leave, how long we have to get where we're going, and when we have to finish our work. The computer orders us to pay our mortgage or car payment or credit card bill; it tells us how much to pay and when to pay it. The company we work for controls what we do with our on-the-job time and how much we get paid for it. Radio and television commercials tell us what to buy, how to look, what to feed our families. And the cleaning—well, everyone knows that the never-ending task of cleaning looms over us like a black cloud. The controlling C list seems almost endless!

No wonder we sometimes feel that we have no control over our lives! While we have this underlying suspicion that we are *supposed* to be in charge, we feel instead like we're at the mercy of our jobs, our schedules, the media, our social groups, our bank accounts, even the demands of our churches or clubs or communities.

Being controlled and manipulated by these creations of man is surely not what God desires for us. The Bible tells us that God's design for us as His children is to "rule over . . . all the earth" (Genesis 1:26). His promise is that we are "more than conquerors through him who loved us" (Romans 8:37).

When you get up in the morning and anticipate another workday, do you feel like a queen, a conqueror? Or do you feel more like a lowly subject in a kingdom dominated by others, where you have little or no control? What has happened to turn the tables so that we feel more like the ruled than the rulers? Did each of us, at some point, trade away our birthright for some kind of worldly gain?

I don't think so. I don't think any of us ever intentionally trades away our inheritance of sovereignty. Instead, we allow it to erode gradually as we accumulate more and more responsibilities and allow more and more controlling influences to creep into our lives. We let the opinions or expectations of others take priority over our most basic values. We let the pressures of the workplace supersede our pursuit of a balanced life. We let the desire for more material possessions dictate our job and lifestyle choices. Losing our God-given dominion is a gradual process, and we progressively find ourselves feeling controlled instead of feeling *in* control.

Regaining sovereignty in our own lives is an act of will, the consequence of a decision to return all aspects of our lives to God's control and to restore Christ's place of lordship in our lives. After all, we have sovereignty over the earth and all that is in it only because God chooses to give it. Apart from Him, we haven't the strength or the power to withstand the worldly forces that threaten to rule us.

All the things that surround us — whether nature's creations or manmade inventions like cars and computers — are only resources. The same is true of gifts that God makes available to us: time, talent, experience, work, insight. All of these are for us to use or not use, as we choose; they are only tools. Whether they rule us or we rule them depends not on them but on us and on how we view our place in the universe.

We become ruled instead of rulers only when we let ourselves live as subjects of the world rather than as children of God. When we choose to accept our sovereign inheritance as God's most precious creation, made and empowered by Him to reign over His world (both this and the next), then we are free to use both the natural and the manmade things of this world for the good of His Kingdom.

One of the great mysteries of faith is that we receive this inheritance of sovereignty only when we are first willing to accept Christ's command of servanthood.

We begin to rule only when we commit ourselves wholly to serve. But our sovereignty is sure: "How much more will those who receive God's abundant provision of grace and of the gift of righteousness reign in life through the one man, Jesus Christ" (Romans 5:17).

PRAYER

Lord, I want to reclaim my role as Your child, Your representative in the world. Free me from the sense of domination by the world's forces, the pressures, the mechanics of daily living, the unrealistic expectations, and the unimportant demands. Help me to serve, so that I may rule with You. Amen.

FIVE

What's a Woman to Do?

*"Martha, Martha," the Lord answered, "you
are worried and upset about many things,
but only one thing is needed. Mary
has chosen what is better, and it will not
be taken away from her."*

Luke 10:41-42

Are you a list-maker? I've learned over the years that keeping a to-do list, both at work and at home, helps me be sure I meet deadlines and don't forget things I need to do.

Part of a typical working woman's to-do list might look like this:

- Take cat to veterinarian.
- Send get-well card to Aunt Mary.
- Call bank about checking account mix-up.
- Buy pantyhose.
- Review Bible study lesson.
- Call electrician about stove.
- Iron blouse for Tuesday meeting.

And that list covers only 4:30 to 5:30 p.m.!

Does this sound familiar? The amazing fact is that, on any given day, most of us face a to-do list like this *in addition to* an eight-hour day at work—which, of course, has its own to-do list.

We have so much to do. I find it very, very easy to identify with the biblical Martha who, the Bible tells us, became pretty stressed out about the fact that Jesus was coming to her house. I'll bet she had a to-do list a mile long. The Bible tells us she was "distracted by all the preparations that had to be made" (Luke 10:40). In fact, she felt so pressured by all her household tasks that she actually asked Jesus to intercede when she saw her sister Mary wasn't helping at all. Mary was just sitting at Jesus' feet, listening to Him.

Jesus' admonition to Martha is also an admonition to us in our hectic, list-ridden lives. "You are worried and upset about many things," Jesus told her, "but only one thing is needed" (Luke 10:41-42). Mary had chosen that one thing: to listen to Jesus.

Sometimes we mistake busyness for god-liness. We feel that if we are running our-selves ragged doing things for our families because we love them, then we are doing God's will. We feel that if we constantly work extra hours on the job, showing that we're conscientious and industrious, we are doing God's will. We believe that if we always say yes when the church needs us to do something, then we are doing God's will.

I'm not sure that we are. Perhaps it is the Martha in us who wants to do all these things. And sometimes that bustling Martha elbows out the gentle Mary in us — that part of us that wants to rest and be quiet and listen to Jesus, to hear His gentle, reassuring voice. That part of us wants to sense His encouraging guidance when we don't know what to do, to feel His loving touch when we feel unloved and unlovable, to know His assurance of forgiveness when we've sinned. The Mary in us seeks His promise of strength when we're tempted and turns to His patient instruction when we desperately need wisdom. But we can't hear Him if the part of us that is like Martha is distracted by our many to-do's.

Of course, we can't just sit back, do nothing, and disregard the commitments we've made. We have to do what it takes to function in our day-to-day lives, to care for others, and to fulfill our employer's expectations. However, maybe we need to give our own to-do lists a little less priority and the Bible's to-do lists a little more. With the help of God's Word, we can prioritize the tasks ahead of us instead of taking on an impossibly long list. Maybe we can even eliminate some tasks that aren't really very important and substitute some that are more in keeping with what truly matters to us.

The to-do list Jesus gives us, for example, really isn't very long (Matthew 22:37,39). In fact, it contains only two items:

■ Love the Lord your God with all your heart and with all your soul and with all your mind.
■ Love your neighbor as yourself.

And how about this short list from Deuteronomy 10:12-13?

■ Fear the Lord.
■ Walk in all His ways.
■ Love Him.
■ Serve Him with all your heart and soul.
■ Observe His commands.

The Scriptures are full of glorious, inspiring, and infinitely challenging to-do lists that can help us fashion our day-to-day lives. For example, Deuteronomy 11:18-21, Psalm 15, and Romans 12:9-21 all contain directions for the way God would have us to live. By giving these to-do lists top priority, we can bring our earthly lists under control and into focus. When we do that, we can come closer to living the lives we really want—and that God wants for us.

PRAYER

Lord, help me to balance the Martha and the Mary in me. Give me the discernment to know when my many to-do's have distracted my focus from You. Give me the quietness of spirit to hear Your voice—no matter how much I have to do. Amen.

SIX

Oops!
I Forgot!

Otherwise, when you eat and are satisfied,
when you build fine houses and settle down, . . .
then your heart will become proud and you
will forget the LORD your God.

Deuteronomy 8:12,14

LET'S SLOW DOWN TODAY TO...

ᘒᕉ *remember what God has done for us;*

ᘒᕉ *cultivate a spirit of God-centered thankfulness;*

ᘒᕉ *exercise Christian stewardship of our God-given capabilities.*

H ow good are you at remembering things? Here's a little test.

1. Where are your car keys right now?
2. What was the name of the school you attended in third grade?
3. When is your boss's birthday?
4. How much did you pay for your last pizza?
5. What is your license plate number?
6. When does your library card expire?
7. What year did the Japanese attack Pearl Harbor?
8. What was the name of your high

school English teacher your sopho-
more year?

9. What group recorded the hit song
"I Wanna Hold Your Hand," and
what year was it?
10. Where did you go on vacation in
1973?
11. What appointments or deadlines
are on your desk calendar for
tomorrow? (No peeking.)
12. The last time you went to lunch
with a coworker, what did he or she
order?

How did you do? Give yourself a point
for each item you could answer with certainty.

Now look at which questions you could
answer and which you couldn't. Can you
remember your English teacher's name but
not where your car keys are? Can you remember your license number but not your boss's
birthday? Can you remember what your
friend ordered for lunch but not whether
you have a meeting tomorrow?

All of us have selective memories. We
remember certain things much better than
others, based on what is important to us,
what else we have on our minds at the time,
what reminders we have to help us remember that particular bit of information, and

other factors. For example, I am more likely to remember that I went to North Carolina on vacation in 1973 because I have a framed souvenir postcard from there.

From a spiritual standpoint, though, human beings tend to be pretty forgetful. It's interesting that this human quality of forgetfulness is reiterated frequently in Scripture, particularly in relation to forgetting what God has done for *us*. This is especially easy to do when we spend so much of our time in the workplace, which revolves around human accomplishments.

In the workplace, the efforts of men and women are translated into dollars, and people are rewarded accordingly. If you do the job that is expected of you, you receive your paycheck. If you excel and prove yourself to be exceptionally capable and dedicated, you receive a promotion. If you make an effort above and beyond the norm, you may receive a bonus or an award or recognition of some other kind. Since it all depends on human effort, we can easily begin to believe that everything we have or achieve or accumulate comes to us through our own power.

God warned the Israelites of this very danger: "You may say to yourself, 'My power and the strength of my hands have produced this wealth for me.' But remember the LORD your God, for it is he who gives you the ability to produce wealth" (Deuteronomy 8:17-18).

As Christians in the workplace, we face the challenge of remembering God's graciousness in the midst of this humanistic environment. We are challenged to remember what God has done for us, rather than viewing accomplishment as something we have done for ourselves.

This challenge of remembering is closely related to the discipline of stewardship. God gives us talents and abilities to use for His glory and for obtaining the necessities in our lives. The workplace is one setting in which we exercise these abilities. Yet those around us may not acknowledge the true source of our talents and skills. They see only that we are capable of certain things, and they reward us accordingly. It's up to us to maintain a godly perspective, remembering that these gifts are from God and are not generated by ourselves.

Cultivating a spirit of thankfulness can help us keep a balanced perspective on our work-related accomplishments. As we acknowledge God as the true source of our abilities, we can avoid the pitfall of overestimating our own power and achievement.

Here's a spiritual exercise to try. The next time someone compliments you on a job well done, or you finish a big project or complete some work that you're especially proud of, take a moment to thank God for giving you the ability and the opportunity to do that work. Place it before Him as an offering, a return on His investment in the resources He has made available to you.

PRAYER

God, thank You for the ability and the opportunity You give me to work. May I always be able to present my work to You with pride, knowing that I have made the best possible use of Your resources. Amen.

PART TWO

TOOLS
OF THE TRADE

SEVEN

What Every Working Woman Needs

*May the God of peace . . . equip you
with everything good for doing his will,
and may he work in us what is pleasing
to him, through Jesus Christ.*

Hebrews 13:20-21

L ast year, the office building where I worked burned down. Virtually everything was destroyed. The bank next door generously gave us office space to use from the day of the fire until something else could be arranged.

There we were, all the company's employees in our borrowed office space—with no supplies or equipment. Everything had burned up. We had no pencils, no computers, no calculators or typewriters. No note pads or telephones or file cabinets.

Within a few days, the bank and our regular suppliers provided us with what we needed to get back into operation. But it had been a strange challenge that first day to try to operate a business with no supplies or equipment.

Businesses, whether large or small, rely on certain equipment to keep them in operation. Whether it's a dry-cleaning store with presses and steam-cleaning machines and washers and dryers or a hospital with delicate and complex laser equipment, a business needs to be properly equipped.

In writing to the Ephesian church, the apostle Paul talked about what Christians need to be properly equipped to do battle with the forces of the world. His list includes the "belt of truth," the "breastplate of righteousness," the "shield of faith," the "helmet of salvation," and the "sword of the Spirit" (Ephesians 6:14-17).

What about Christian women in the workplace? What equipment do we need to efficiently and effectively represent Christ to those around us? Here's a checklist to consider.

REQUIRED EQUIPMENT
A bookshelf. Our place of work must have space for God's Word. The Bible is our operator's manual, no matter what kind of work we do. It's more important than the employee handbook, the departmental procedures manual, or even that little brochure

on "What to Do in an Emergency." We *must* find a place for God's Word in our hearts and in our workplaces if we are to be truly "on the job" for Him.

A scale. We need to weigh the things we say and do before we say and do them. Are they in keeping with Christ's example? Will they glorify God and bring good to others?

A wastebasket. We will be better off if we throw away old hurts, lingering disappointments, petty frustrations, and day-to-day irritations to keep them from cluttering up our minds and wasting our energy. The wastebasket is also the best place to file the unforgiving feelings that strain our on-the-job relationships.

A mirror. Checking for planks in our own eyes (Matthew 7:3) helps us avoid concentrating on the shortcomings and failings of others.

A postage stamp. We need to be stamped and sealed by the Holy Spirit to be on our way as Christ's letters (2 Corinthians 3:3) to an unbelieving world. Through us, the Holy Spirit brings Christ's message and His example to those around us. Are we letters bursting with good news and hope for the people with whom we work, or are we stamped "Insufficient postage" because we're too busy to do His work?

A piggy bank. The Bible calls us to set aside a part of our earnings for God's use. Throughout history, God's mandate to His people has been to provide for the needs of the poor, the hungry, the sick, the homeless. Those of us with the ability to work have the obligation to share with those who cannot meet their own needs.

A balloon. When day-to-day concerns and pressures threaten to weigh us down, we need something to lift our hearts to a higher plane. A balloon reminds us that we are "strangers on earth" (Psalm 119:19), not bound by the world's limitations.

A measuring cup. As Christians, our goal is not to measure how much we are getting from others, but to be sure that we are giving to them "a good measure, pressed down, shaken together and running over" (Luke 6:38).

A pair of running shoes. We must stay in the race. There is an urgency about God's work. We cannot wait until someone else does it, or until it's convenient, or until we have become such spiritual giants or biblical scholars that we have all the answers. The time for action is now, and we are to run—not walk—as we go about the work of His Kingdom.

An alarm clock. Sleeping on the job is tempting. "So then, let us not be like others, who are asleep, but let us be alert and self-controlled" (1 Thessalonians 5:6).

There is work to be done. Let's be fully equipped for the job!

PRAYER

God, I thank You for the challenge of doing Your work. Thank You for entrusting to me the mission of representing You in my place of work. I pray that You will equip me well and teach me to rely on Your strength and Your guidance. Amen.

EIGHT

Using the Round File

*A man's wisdom gives him patience;
it is to his glory to overlook an offense.*

Proverbs 19:11

LET'S SLOW DOWN TODAY TO...

۶۰ *free ourselves from the burden of old hurts and resentments;*

۶۰ *practice the skill of overlooking an offense.*

Have you ever heard the expression "Put it in the round file"? The first time a boss ever instructed me to file something in the round file, I had no idea what he meant. What "round file"? All I had in my office was a standard four-drawer filing cabinet. Was there some piece of office equipment I was missing? Or was the round file some computer file? If it was, no one had told me the password!

The *round file*, of course, is a workplace expression for the wastebasket. The upcoming generation of working people may find it hard to understand, since most office-type wastebaskets are now rectangular. But we old-timers know that they used to be round. The old gray metal ones about eighteen inches in diameter could hold a lot of mistakes.

Since I've spent most of my career doing writing of one kind or another, I grew to appreciate those roomy wastebaskets. There's a certain grim satisfaction in knowing that you can glibly dispose of your mistakes by tossing crumpled-up pieces of paper into a waiting container; there's a certain confidence in knowing that it will always have room for one more. And every night, an invisible office-cleaning crew would come and cart away all the trash, leaving me an empty wastebasket to fill with the next day's rejected words. Otherwise, my coworkers might have come in some morning to find me buried under a mountain of crumpled-up sheets of typing paper, gasping for air and frantically trying to dig my way out!

None of the Bible translations I have contain the word *wastebasket* or even the expression *round file*, but I firmly believe that the Scriptures call us to be equipped with a roomy spiritual wastebasket. This invaluable piece of equipment enables us, through Christ's forgiveness, to dispose of the waste paper of past offenses—not only our own, but also those that we believe others have committed against us. It keeps this workplace trash from cluttering up our lives and interfering with our on-the-job relationships.

In other words, it enables us to clear our spiritual desks of old hurts and resentments and unkind slights from others—all those nagging little recollections that, if we file them away, gradually erode our relationships. We cannot maintain positive, enjoyable, effective working relationships with people if we constantly hold their past offenses against them.

Maybe a coworker said something in a fit of temper or a bout of sarcasm and we were embarrassed. If we keep that memory lingering in our spiritual in-basket every day, then we'll remember that moment and feel humiliated and angry all over again every time we see that person. We won't be able to rebuild that relationship until we dispose of that old hurt.

Maybe the boss made us work over a weekend when we had made elaborate plans to go camping with friends, and we had to cancel at the last minute. Sure, it was disappointing. But if that old feeling of disappointment and resentment comes back to work with us each day, it will color our whole job outlook negatively.

We need to take time each day to crumple

up those old offenses and put them in the round file. Then we can leave them for the Holy Spirit's cleaning crew to cart away, freeing us from the clutter they create in our hearts and minds. We won't have to worry about being buried under a mountain of stored-up hurts and resentments.

Besides interfering with our ability to have a Christlike attitude toward others, the accumulation of workplace trash also hinders our overall spiritual growth. We cannot "ascend to the hill of the LORD" (Psalm 24:3) if we carry along with us the accumulated offenses we haven't been able to forgive. Try this exercise in imagination:

Estimate the quantity of trash that you've deposited in your workplace wastebasket over the past five years. Now picture yourself loading all of that into a huge trash bag — or several huge trash bags if necessary. Now picture yourself starting to climb a mountain while carrying all that trash along with you. If your mental picture is like mine, the imaginary you can hardly move!

The Christian life is a continuous, gradual climb to spiritual heights. It taxes every part of our being to the limit as we seek to grow and learn and follow Christ's example, drawing on the Holy Spirit for strength and encouragement.

Let's not make that climb harder for ourselves by toting along the burdensome baggage of an unforgiving spirit. Instead, let's use our spiritual wastebaskets. Let's practice the skill of overlooking an offense until we can do it easily and confidently — and permanently.

PRAYER

God, You have forgiven me so much. I thank You that I don't have to carry along the burden of my own past sins. Help me to forgive others in the same way, not harboring anger and resentment, but overlooking day-to-day offenses so that I can focus on becoming more like You. Amen.

NINE

Call Out the Guards!

*Discretion will protect you,
and understanding will guard you.*

Proverbs 2:11

```
┌─────────────────────────────────────┐
│  ╔═══════════════════════════════╗  │
│  ║  LET'S SLOW DOWN TODAY TO...   ║  │
│  ╠═══════════════════════════════╣  │
│  ║                               ║  │
│  ║   ∂➤ reflect on the biblical  ║  │
│  ║  quality of discretion;       ║  │
│  ║   ∂➤ learn to exercise        ║  │
│  ║  discretion in the            ║  │
│  ║  things we say and do.        ║  │
│  ║                               ║  │
│  ╚═══════════════════════════════╝  │
└─────────────────────────────────────┘
```

LET'S SLOW DOWN TODAY TO...

∂➤ *reflect on the biblical quality of discretion;*

∂➤ *learn to exercise discretion in the things we say and do.*

Laura was a college student who worked in my office last summer. One day she came to work looking very distressed. When I asked her what was wrong, she poured out the following story:

Laura and her parents were hosting a family of house guests from another country. Laura's father had met this family through a business connection in their country, and he had invited them to come to Florida for a visit. Everything had gone reasonably well for the first few days.

"Then, yesterday," Laura told me, "these people were sitting around the house and talking. I was doing some work in my room, so they probably didn't think I could hear them; and even if I could, they probably thought I wouldn't be able to understand their language.

"What they didn't know was that I'm bilingual. I understood every word. All they did was criticize my family, our house, and even this country. Listening to them, I was just heartbroken for my parents, who had worked so hard to make their visit enjoyable. I was so angry and hurt I don't know what to do. I never did let them know I had understood."

Laura's guests obviously believed that the language barrier would prevent their thoughtless and unkind words from reaching Laura and her family. But it didn't.

Did you know that the Bible offers us protection from the painful consequences of our own unkind, thoughtless, and sinful words and actions? It does! That protective gift is called discretion.

Discretion is a quality closely akin to such traits as wisdom, prudence, and the sober judgment mentioned in Romans 12:3. The woman of discretion is able to make wise and careful choices about the things she says and does—*before* she says or does them! That's how discretion can protect us from painful consequences. It prevents us from doing or saying the things that produce those consequences. It gives us the ability to exercise Christlike judgment before we choose to say or do things that might bring unhappiness or hurt to ourselves and/or others. If Laura's guests had exercised discretion instead of hiding behind the presumed language barrier, they never would have said the unkind things that she found so hurtful.

Think how beneficial discretion can be in a workplace setting. When we hear the latest tidbit of office gossip, discretion guards us from repeating it. When the boss's unfair criticism makes us see red, discretion helps us make wise choices about how to deal with the situation. It keeps us from saying something in anger that might jeopardize our jobs or our relationships with our bosses. When we become privy to confidential information, whether it's a routine part of the job or just something we overhear, discretion dictates to us the trustworthy and responsible stewardship of that information.

King David recognized the importance of discretion. Although he, like all of us, lacked it on certain occasions, it was one of the qualities he bequeathed to his son Solomon, as he became king of Israel. Invoking God's blessing, David said to Solomon, "May the LORD give you discretion and understanding when he puts you in command over Israel, so that you may keep the law of the LORD your God" (1 Chronicles 22:12).

One of the most entertaining descriptions in the Bible depicts for us a woman who lacks discretion: "Like a gold ring in a pig's snout is a beautiful woman who shows no discretion" (Proverbs 11:22). Why is discretion so important? Because it helps protect us from unpleasant consequences of rash words and actions. It keeps us from looking as ridiculous as a gold ring in a pig's snout!

There are other benefits, too:

The discreet woman is trustworthy. People know that she can be trusted with their confidences, because she has the judgment and self-control not to repeat things that she is told in confidence. She chooses her words carefully and knows when it's time not to speak at all.

The discreet woman is forward-looking. She weighs the consequences of what she is about to say or do. She avoids making sudden judgments, spur-of-the-moment decisions, and emotional choices without reflecting on their impact.

The discreet woman is sensitive to other people. She understands that everything she says and does affects others. She considers *their* feelings, *their* needs, and *their* welfare, and she weighs her words and actions in light of those things.

Discretion needs to be standard equipment in any workplace!

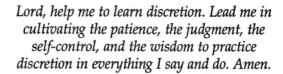

PRAYER

Lord, help me to learn discretion. Lead me in cultivating the patience, the judgment, the self-control, and the wisdom to practice discretion in everything I say and do. Amen.

TEN

Beautiful
You

*Charm is deceptive, and beauty is fleeting; but
a woman who fears the LORD is to be praised.*

Proverbs 31:30

LET'S SLOW DOWN TODAY TO...

≥ *consider the role that physical beauty plays in our lives;*

≥ *study a biblical example of a truly beautiful woman.*

When you buy a women's magazine, don't you love to look at the "before" and "after" pictures in the articles about beauty makeovers? Of course, I'm convinced that they take the "before" pictures right after those women get up in the morning. No wonder they look better "after"! But it still amazes me how much a woman's appearance can be changed by the skillful work of makeup artists and hairdressers.

Nearly all of us would probably like to be more attractive than we are. We want to feel good about how we look, both to ourselves and to others. Our awareness of beauty is heightened, too, because our culture puts such a premium on physical attractiveness. Everywhere we turn there's a beautiful model smiling out of a magazine cover or a television set or a movie screen. By comparison, we suddenly feel plain or dowdy or fat or skinny or just plain flawed. When the company hires a new woman to work in our department, we size her up to see whether she's more attractive than we are. Constantly evaluating how we measure up to the world's standards, we scrutinize our own (and other women's) hair, clothes, facial features, makeup, and bodies.

The perils of constantly comparing ourselves to others and the dangers of letting jealousy get a grip on us are very real problems for working women. The work environment fosters competition in many areas — money, power, and prestige, and even personal appearance. In such a competition-charged setting, it's especially important for us as Christian women to maintain a balanced and biblical perspective on physical beauty and outward appearance.

Does God's design for Christian women, then, call for us to look like the "before" pictures in the magazines? Is it wrong for us to make any effort to make ourselves attractive?

On the contrary. God's Word indicates

that He wants us to be beautiful. Certainly Solomon's Song of Songs celebrates womanly beauty. Like so many things — wealth, power, sex, and success, beauty is neither good nor evil in itself. Whether beauty hinders or enhances our calling as Christian women depends on how we feel about it, how we use it, what we're willing to do to have it, and what priority we place on it.

Let's see what we can learn about beauty from the example of Esther, one of the Bible's most beautiful women.

Even in the ancient days of the Persian Empire, beauty was honored. It was Esther's beauty that gave her access to the palace of King Xerxes and won her the position of queen. The Bible tells us she was "lovely in form and features" (Esther 2:7). Out of all the young women brought to the king from throughout his vast kingdom, "the king was attracted to Esther more than to any of the other women, and she won his favor and approval" (2:17). In fact, "Esther won the favor of everyone who saw her" (2:15). She must have been beautiful indeed.

When Esther's cousin Mordecai came and told her of Haman's plot to destroy the Jews, he urged her to use her position and her standing with the king to thwart Haman's evil intentions. Mordecai challenged her with these words: "And who knows but that you have come to royal position for such a time as this?" (4:14). She was the only one in a position to save her people. Her beauty was the key to her position; therefore, it became the key to her shrewd and dangerous plan to destroy Haman and save the Jews.

Physical beauty was a tool that enabled Esther to be in the right place at the right time to carry out her crucial task for God's people. But it was her inner qualities of courage, loyalty, faith, compassion, and wisdom that enabled her to fulfill her mission. Without those qualities, she surely would not have been willing to take the risks she did, to execute such a difficult plan, or to assume such an overwhelming responsibility.

God gives each of us different abilities, talents, and opportunities to carry out His work. Physical beauty, by the world's standards, is a tool that He gives to some and not to others. It is no more than that, and no less.

Esther has gone down in history as one of the great women of God, not because she was beautiful, but because she was willing to use whatever she had to carry out the work of saving God's people from destruction.

Whether we have been given her kind of beauty or not, are we willing to use whatever gifts we do have for the glory of God and the good of His people?

ELEVEN

101 Ways to Use a Gift

Be very careful, then, how you live — not as unwise but as wise, making the most of every opportunity, because the days are evil.

Ephesians 5:15-16

> ❧ *examine our own motives in relation to beauty;*
>
> ❧ *reflect on how we will use the gifts we have been given.*

Christine was an exceptionally attractive young woman who worked as the receptionist for an advertising agency. She enjoyed her job; she liked meeting interesting people and working in a fast-paced environment.

Recently, the office was buzzing with talk about how badly the agency wanted to land a big new account, Harris Manufacturing. The staff was putting all their time and energy into developing a presentation that would be sure to win the account for their agency. Everything had to be ready by Wednesday the twelfth, when Mr. Harris, the founder and owner of the manufacturing company, was coming to look over the agency. At the end of his visit, he'd decide whether or not he wanted them to do his company's advertising.

Don, Christine's boss, asked her to come into his office about a week before Mr. Harris was due to arrive.

"Christine," Don began, "as you know, we've all put a lot of work into getting ready for the presentation to Mr. Harris. I've planned some social events during his visit, too, just so he'll see that our agency knows how to treat our clients well.

"I've planned a small dinner party on Wednesday night to give Mr. Harris a chance to meet some of our other big clients. I thought it would be nice, since his wife isn't coming with him, if someone would kind of keep him company at the party. You've been with the agency for a couple of years now, and I thought you would be a good person to take on that responsibility. If Mr. Harris has a good time during his visit here, it could mean a great deal to all of us here at the agency. You're not busy Wednesday night, are you?"

■

The New Testament tells us a story of another beautiful woman whose name is Salome. (See Matthew 14:6-12 and Mark 6:14-29.) When the beautiful Salome danced for her uncle, King Herod, and many of his friends at a lavish birthday party he gave to honor himself, Herod was captivated by her performance—so much so that he told her he would give her anything she wanted, up to half of his kingdom. Not sure what to ask for, she consulted her mother, who saw an opportunity to rid herself of an irritating prophet who objected to her plan to marry the king.

The rest is history. Egged on by her mother, Salome requested the head of John the Baptist—and she got it.

Now what do a receptionist in a modern-day advertising agency and a beautiful teenage dancer in AD 29 have in common? They both have been given a choice: whether or not to let their beauty be used for an immoral, dishonest, or unethical purpose. Just as Esther had the opportunity to use her beauty, Salome and Christine both had opportunities to use their beauty also—but not for good. Christine's boss wanted to use her beauty to influence Mr. Harris's business judgment (in his wife's absence) instead of letting the agency win the account on its own merits. Salome's mother wanted to use her daughter's beauty to get revenge on someone who stood between her and her self-serving ambition.

We don't have to be show-stopping beauties like Esther, Christine, and Salome to find ourselves in the same dilemma. Toward what goals are we willing to let our physical appearance be used—by us or by others? As we try out that new lipstick or put on that great new outfit in the morning, it's helpful to reflect on why we're willing to invest so much time, effort, and money in making ourselves more physically attractive.

Is it because we respect ourselves, enjoy our femininity, and want to present a positive appearance as Christ's ambassadors? Or is it because we're determined to look better than that coworker in the sales department who always seems to be one-upping us? Is it to show that we care about our jobs and, therefore, about the image we present for the company? Or is it to make up for the fact that we don't feel good about our personality or our ability, so we want to use our appearance to outshine others? Or is our goal perhaps to stir up a little romantic interest from that good-looking accountant in the finance department—who just happens to be married?

Like Esther, Christine, and Salome, we have choices about how we will use the tools we have been given. Whether the tools in question are physical attractiveness, talent, position, influence, knowledge, ability, or any other assets, God calls us to be careful how we use them.

PRAYER

God, we have so many choices to make. Help me to reaffirm to You my role as a living sacrifice, to commit all that I am to Your use. Give me the strength to resist the world's pressure to use my gifts for evil ends. Amen.

TWELVE

The Eye of the Beholder

Your beauty should not come from outward adornment, such as braided hair and the wearing of gold jewelry and fine clothes. Instead, it should be that of your inner self, the unfading beauty of a gentle and quiet spirit, which is of great worth in God's sight.

1 Peter 3:3-4

▪ *define the kind of beauty God wants for us;*

▪ *determine the source of real inward and outward beauty.*

The Scottish poet Robert Burns once expressed the wish that God would give each of us the gift "to see ourselves as others see us." If you were offered that gift right now, would you take it? What do you think you would see?

Being able to see ourselves through the eyes of others would surely be a mixed blessing. There's a good chance we'd see things we'd rather not; and, at the same time, we'd probably see some things that would encourage and affirm us.

So much of the time and money we spend to make ourselves more attractive is geared to making us look better to others. Yet I suspect that in reality no one but us really notices the magnificent mauve lipstick, the midnight mania eye shadow, or the precious pink blusher.

If we could truly "see ourselves as others see us," we would see a composite of each person's experiences with us. We could then view the inner person that has been revealed to them through the things we've said and done and the way we've said and done them.

The Bible admonishes us to dress and behave appropriately as Christian women: "I also want women to dress modestly, with decency and propriety, not with braided hair or gold or pearls or expensive clothes, but with good deeds, appropriate for women who profess to worship God" (1 Timothy 2:9-10). We cannot escape the reality that our deeds affect how others perceive us — whether they see us as beautiful or not-so-beautiful.

Certainly the Bible emphasizes the beauty of the inner person rather than the outward appearance. All the cosmetics and fashions in the world can't reveal the beauty of Christ to others; only the words, attitudes, and actions of a Christ-centered life can do that. Nor can cosmetics conceal an uncharitable or worldly spirit.

The true inner beauty that Christ gives

does show on the outside. The magnetic and captivating power of this inner beauty is very real, not just something our mothers promise us when we complain that we're plain or have a big nose or are too fat or too short. All of us know people who simply radiate kindness, patience, compassion, and other beautiful qualities of the spirit. Those qualities even show in their faces, in expressions that reflect peace or joy or wisdom. Others are automatically drawn to these people, because they know that these individuals will treat them with kindness, gentleness, and respect. In a harsh and competitive world, who wouldn't want to be around someone like that?

Are these individuals outwardly attractive by the world's standards? Maybe so. Maybe not. The point is that it doesn't matter. The beauty that draws others to them transcends anything from the cosmetic counter or fashion magazines.

The prophet Isaiah, in predicting the coming of the Messiah, forewarned us that He would not be beautiful or magnificent by the world's standards: "He had no beauty or majesty to attract us to him, nothing in his appearance that we should desire him" (Isaiah 53:2). Yet when Christ finally came, people walked for miles just to see Him, to be near Him, touch Him, even just to grasp at His coat. He was beautiful in their eyes.

In the passage at the beginning of this chapter, the apostle Paul lists two qualities that can help us as Christian women to cultivate this inner beauty that can be outwardly seen.

Gentleness. Gentleness is one of the characteristics of the fruit of the Spirit Paul listed in Galatians 5:23, and its importance as an element of Christian character is reemphasized throughout Scripture. Gentleness is a way of dealing with others. It shows in the way we express our opinions, resolve conflict, and handle ourselves under pressure. Gentleness is the quality that prevents us from being harsh or punitive or self-seeking, even when we are stressed or angry. The gentle spirit doesn't always need to win, even at the expense of others.

You can be sure, though, that gentleness is not a weakness of character, but a strength. Proverbs 25:15 tells us, "A gentle tongue can break a bone." Christ was gentle. He wants us be gentle, too.

Quietness of spirit. Peter coupled gentleness with a quiet spirit. This quietness of spirit is akin to serenity, a deep-seated peace that comes from knowing we are in God's care.

We can also see this quietness as the opposite of restlessness. It frees us from the world's constant striving to prove we are more worthwhile or smarter or more talented than someone else. It means being quietly confident of our own uniqueness and value, while those caught up in the world's values clamor to prove themselves. Our worth was proved when Christ died for us. We experience His quiet grace in every day we live for Him.

PRAYER

Lord, I want to have the kind of beauty that draws others to Christ. Help me to cultivate the inward qualities of gentleness and quietness, and give me the strength to do the good things I know I should do, so that others will see You in me. Amen.

THIRTEEN

Where's the Rest?

But those who hope in the LORD will renew their strength. They will soar on wings like eagles; they will run and not grow weary, they will walk and not be faint.

Isaiah 40:31

LET'S SLOW DOWN TODAY TO...

❧ *examine some causes of chronic fatigue in our lives;*

❧ *accept the rest that Christ offers.*

Rosemary got up this morning at 6:30, her usual time. She got dressed for work, grabbed a cup of coffee, made sure there was cereal on the table for the kids, left them a note reminding them to feed the cat and not miss the school bus, and headed out the door.

During her morning at work she finished the last-minute arrangements for a board meeting, processed the usual stacks of paperwork, resolved a misunderstanding between two of her coworkers, made thirteen phone calls, and dealt with the miscellaneous bits and pieces of work that came across her desk.

On her lunch hour, she shopped for a

wedding present for her nephew, picked up the dry cleaning, and then zipped through the drive-up window at Burger Bonanza. She spent the afternoon troubleshooting clients' problems, attending the monthly meeting of the employee governance committee, and pulling together the data for a marketing report that's due next week.

On her way home at the end of the day, she picked up some groceries and dropped off a few books at the library. She fixed spaghetti and a salad for the family for dinner, listened to her thirteen-year-old daughter's latest tale of teenage heartbreak, and helped her son with his homework.

At long last, she sat on the sofa and was finally ready to leaf through a magazine she picked up at the store. There was an article on time management that she especially wanted to read; but, not surprisingly, she could barely keep her eyes open.

Are your days often like Rosemary's? Mine are. No wonder we feel worn out at the end of the day. But if you're like me, fatigue catches you by surprise and you find yourself saying, "I can't understand why I'm so tired."

When you think about it, though, the cause of our fatigue probably isn't physical. Unless you have a job that requires hard physical activity—like teaching aerobics or working in construction—your job probably isn't physically demanding. Sitting at a desk, which is what I do, isn't. Answering the phone isn't. Data entry isn't. Waiting on customers isn't. But we're still tired.

Why? Let's look at several causes.

Overcommitment. Committing ourselves to more than is realistic or practical for us creates constant pressure and a nagging sense of failure when we can't get everything done. It leads to chronic stress, and ultimately to burnout. From time to time each of us needs to reevaluate the things we're devoting our time to and decide whether those things are truly in keeping with our priorities. We may be spending too much of our time doing things that really aren't important in terms of our most precious life-goals and our highest priorities. Sometimes a large-scale restructuring of how we spend our time is just what the doctor ordered.

Worry. Worrying about finances, the future, our job situation, relationships, and other elements of our lives can simply wear us out. The saddest part is, worry doesn't accomplish anything—*unless* it motivates us to act. I can worry about the state of our environment, or I can recycle, conserve water and energy, and encourage others to do the same.

I can worry that an on-the-job relationship is strained, or I can take the first step toward healing the situation. Jesus tells us point-blank not to worry (Matthew 6:25-34). It's not good for our physical health or our spiritual health.

Neglecting personal needs. We keep our cars in good running order because we depend on them so much; but do we ever consider the routine maintenance needed for our own bodies? How many of us, like Rosemary, grab a cup of coffee for breakfast and fast food for lunch? We often don't get enough sleep or exercise or the nutrients we need for good health. We decide we don't have the time or money for regular medical check-ups, but we find time and money for other things. No wonder we're tired. We abuse our bodies in ways we would never abuse our cars or anything else we have.

God gave us our bodies as the physical homes of our spirits. We don't have the right to treat them with disrespect.

Nor do we have the right to neglect our own spiritual needs. Isaiah tells us that when we rely on God, our strength will be renewed. When our spirits are recharged and revitalized by spending time with God, in prayer and in His word, we tap into endless sources of mental, emotional, and spiritual energy.

At the same time, Jesus promises us rest—rest from overcommitment through the assurance that we do not have to work to earn His love; rest from worry, as we trust in His promise never to forsake us; rest from physical neglect, as we learn to respect and value ourselves as He did.

Fatigue doesn't have to be a way of life for us.

PRAYER

God, teach me to rest in You. Focus my energy into doing the work You have for me in this world, not wasting it by excessive busyness or fruitless worrying or self-neglect. Renew me with the boundless energy of Your Spirit. Amen.

FOURTEEN

A Blast from the Past

Therefore, if anyone is in Christ, he is a new creation; the old has gone, the new has come!

2 Corinthians 5:17

LET'S SLOW DOWN TODAY TO...

❧ *reflect on what we can learn from our experiences;*

❧ *accept God's offer of freedom from past sins, disappointments, and hurts;*

❧ *experience what it means to be new in Christ.*

My friend Brenda started a new job about a year ago. She was talking recently about the influence of each person's past on their present attitudes and behavior and was telling me what she had observed in the process of getting to know her coworkers.

"As I've gotten to know each person better, I've learned a little about their backgrounds by listening to the things they've said about their childhoods, their families, or their past experiences. It's made me see so clearly how much people are a product of their pasts. It really helps me understand why they do the things they do and why they feel the way they do—their attitude toward their work, for example, or how they relate to other people."

The past is so much a part of us. Everything that happens to us from the day we're born—and even in the months before we're born—shapes the adults we will become and influences the paths our lives will take.

For example, Mary's parents were very critical, and they punished her any time she made a mistake—if she spilled her milk, did poorly on an exam, or didn't follow their instructions properly. As a result, she's terrified of taking risks of any kind or trying anything new, for fear she'll make a mistake.

Now, years later, Mary is having trouble moving up in her job and increasing her level of responsibility. Every time there's a new task to be tried or a new way of doing things, she panics and finds ways to avoid doing it. She's just sure she'll be severely criticized if she doesn't get it exactly right the first time.

If you could, which of these would you like to do: (a) relive your past, (b) erase it completely, or (c) change it? Probably most of us would answer "all of the above." Most people have periods or events in their lives that were especially happy or meaningful, that they would like to experience again.

Then there are the episodes we'd like to forget forever—times that were painful or foolish or even tragic. And then, of course, there are those things we did or choices we made that we regret, the ones we wish we could somehow go back and change or at least repair the damage they caused.

We know that the past plays a major role in shaping who we are and even how we perform on the job. But how does it fit into God's plan for us?

God gives us the ability to learn from experience. The age-old axiom that experience is the best teacher certainly seems to have its roots in Scripture. The biblical writer James said that our trials, our painful experiences in life, provide a testing of our faith that ultimately strengthens us. From our difficult experiences we learn perseverance, which according to James, "must finish its work so that [we] may be mature and complete" (James 1:4). Growing in faith through the trying periods and circumstances of our lives is part of God's design for the mature Christian life.

Biblical scholar William Barclay has suggested that this ability to learn from the past is a vital component of spiritual wisdom. James urges us to rely on God to give us wisdom. We can turn to Him to help us reflect on our experiences and discern what they have to teach us. Not only our negative experiences, but our positive ones, too, hold important lessons for us. What important lessons have you learned from your experiences and trials?

God offers us freedom from the past. For some people like Mary, though, the past becomes a crippling burden that keeps them from living freely and fully as God desires. They go through life enslaved by guilt over their mistakes, by resentment over hurts, by self-hatred stemming from perceived failures, and by self-defeating behavior learned from negative experiences. This emotional burden colors everything they do. It prevents happy, healthy relationships. It interferes with successful job performance. It leads to addictions and other destructive behavior.

Through Christ, though, we have God's promise of newness. We can put to death that old creature—the guilt-ridden, angry, defeated person we once were, that person burdened by the baggage of the past. We can literally become a new person, freed by Christ to live in newness and hope.

What is there in your past that weighs you down? Accept God's promise of freedom and start living as His new creation.

PRAYER

Dear God, I thank You for Christ's willing sacrifice to make me free from my past sins and failures so that I can live in newness and hope instead of being crushed by the weight of past mistakes. I thank You, too, for the ability to learn from experience, to grow wiser and stronger in faith through the trials that life brings me. Amen.

FIFTEEN

My Lord, What a Morning!

In the morning, O LORD, you hear my voice;
in the morning I lay my requests
before you and wait in expectation.

Psalm 5:3

≥• *improve the way we approach each day;*

≥• *learn to use our mornings to build a solid foundation for our days.*

I t's Wednesday morning. The alarm goes off; you wake up and groan. You cringe at the prospect of going to work because you know your desk is piled with paperwork a foot high. You argued with a co-worker yesterday, and she's hurt and angry. Now you dread facing her. Your house payment is due. Your son is in a silent-and-surly phase. Instead of crawling out of bed, you wish you could be like those cartoon characters who crawl into a hole and then pull the hole in after them.

Our lives are so hectic. Is it any wonder a day that begins like this doesn't improve much as it wears on?

The psalmist wrote of laying his requests

before God in the morning and waiting in expectation. You can feel his excitement, his sense of anticipation as he looks forward to God's working in his life that day.

How often do we feel this way? Don't our days more often begin with a groan—or a whimper—than a song?

The Bible's promises are an ever-ready antidote to the morning blahs, if only we can remember to make them a part of our morning mindset. Our mornings can be changed from glum to glorious if we learn to bear in mind what God promises each day.

The promise of newness. One of the things that sabotages our mornings failure to make use of the spiritual wastebasket we discussed earlier. We begin each day weighed down by leftover baggage of the day before—the mistakes we made, the arguments we had, the thoughtless or unkind acts or words that we'd give anything if we could take back. Or maybe the baggage we're carrying around is even older—days or months or even years old. It's hard to greet a day with joy when we're emotionally, spiritually, and mentally burdened with old hurts and sins.

One of the clearest promises in Scripture is the promise of newness. All we have to do is to reach out for it, to ask for God's forgiveness, and to allow ourselves to be renewed by His love and grace. Christ makes us new creatures. Our old sins are forgiven. The slate is wiped clean of our past mistakes. When we start our mornings with this sense of newness, each day is indeed a brand new gift of twenty-four hours in which to experience the abundant life God promises us.

No matter what leftovers we are carrying, God has the power to renew us if we only ask Him: "I will give them an undivided heart and put a new spirit in them" (Ezekiel 11:19).

The promise of strength. Sometimes, as we look ahead to our day, we feel that we simply don't have the strength to do all that will be demanded of us. Another day of coping with our problems and concerns just isn't a very appealing prospect. We feel like the stress of our jobs may break us like a rubber band pulled too tight. Our emotional, financial, spiritual, or physical concerns sap our energy, and we feel tired at just the thought of another day of dealing with them.

Our own strength often isn't adequate for the challenges facing us. That's why reliance on God is one of the key elements of Christian discipline. The psalmist cries, "But I will sing of your strength, in the morning I will sing of your love; for you are my fortress, my refuge in times of trouble" (Psalm

59:16). Like Isaiah, we must ask the Lord, "Be our strength every morning" (Isaiah 33:2).

The promise of partnership. When you've survived an especially difficult time in your life, or completed a tough project at work, or even won an award, have you ever found yourself telling a friend or loved one, "I could never have made it without you"? The support of another person, working in partnership with us, can help us surmount obstacles we could never overcome alone and can help us achieve things we never would have believed possible. Our days often look their bleakest when we feel that there's no one willing to be our partner, no one who cares about us and will be there to help us through whatever lies ahead.

God promises us His constant partnership, His continual presence at our side. He wants to join with us in meeting the challenges of living Christlike lives in a complex world. We never have to be alone. If we only ask, everything we undertake, whether it's getting through a difficult day or writing a great novel, can be undertaken in partnership with Him.

With Christ dwelling in us, the Holy Spirit guiding us, and God's loving presence surrounding us, surely nothing our days might hold can overcome us. We can sing with David, "Let the morning bring me word of your unfailing love, for I have put my trust in you. Show me the way I should go, for to you I lift up my soul" (Psalm 143:8).

PRAYER

❧

Lord, You have given me so much cause for rejoicing in the start of each new day. Fill me with the joy of Your presence when I awaken, and remind me of Your love throughout every moment. Amen.

SIXTEEN

Good Night

*By day the LORD directs his love,
at night his song is with me – a prayer
to the God of my life.*

Psalm 42:8

LET'S SLOW DOWN TODAY TO...

- *find some new ways to bring our days to a close;*
- *cultivate a truly restful spirit.*

A few years ago, I visited my doctor to seek her advice about a minor illness. The symptoms were always the worst when I woke up in the morning, which meant that my days got off to a pretty uncomfortable start.

The doctor prescribed some medicine I was supposed to take every night before I went to bed. When I got home that first night, I took the medicine as she had directed and was delighted to find that I felt fine when I woke up the next morning.

For some reason, though, as time went on, I frequently forgot to take the medicine at bedtime. As a result, I continued to wake up feeling ill many mornings.

Looking back, I marvel at my own irresponsibility. All I had to do to cure my illness was to take the medicine as prescribed. But instead, for some reason, I often elected to ignore the doctor's simple advice, and I continued to experience the unpleasant symptoms.

We sometimes operate the same way in our spiritual lives. Instead of spending some time in prayer and fellowship with God at the end of the day to ensure a peaceful night's rest and a good start on the next day, we leave our spiritual "medicine" on the night stand and take all the day's ills to bed with us. The result is often a fitful night, filled with churning thoughts that make rest impossible. We are like the man whose days are described in Ecclesiastes: "All his days his work is pain and grief; even at night his mind does not rest" (2:23).

As we know, God's promises can help get our days off to a good start. Now let's see how we can bring those days to a peaceful and prayerful close.

Commit our cares to God. Unless we let go of our worries and concerns, they will fill our minds and hearts all night, keeping us from the physical and emotional rest we need. Stewing and fretting over them all night will not do us any good anyway. Instead, we are told, "Cast your cares on the LORD and he will sustain you; he will never let the righteous fall" (Psalm 55:22).

This letting go is sometimes much harder than it sounds. We may say, "Lord, I'm entrusting this problem to You," but then we treat it like a yo-yo, snatching it back from God and worrying about it off and on all during the night. If you tend to do this, try to take some physical action that symbolizes turning your cares over to God. Keep a note pad by your bed, and write down all your concerns. Then, once you've written down your worries on a piece of paper, crumple it up and throw it away. Or fill a glass with water and let it sit on your night stand while you get ready for bed. Then, right before you retire, pour the water into the sink and watch it drain away.

Thank God for the day's good things. Learn to focus on good things—the kind words of a coworker or praise from a boss; an unexpected hug from a child; a letter from a friend; an exercise class that left you feeling refreshed; or a verse of Scripture that encouraged you. Even on our worst days, we have much for which to thank Him. Cultivating a spirit of thankfulness refocuses our sight and helps us to see blessings rather than trials.

Seek God's guidance in decision-making. Facing difficult decisions is a sure sleep-robber. We lie awake, going over and over the pros and cons of our various options. We weigh the consequences of each choice. We even try to see into the future, to anticipate what will happen if we choose option A or option B or option C.

When we ask God for His guidance, we feel less alone. We can quit struggling so hard with the limitations of our own wisdom. We can draw upon the Holy Spirit to "teach us all things" and remind us of what Jesus taught us (John 14:26). The decision will still be waiting for us the next morning, but we can sleep peacefully, knowing that we won't be making it alone.

Ask God's forgiveness. As we have learned, the burden of unforgiven sins is a heavy one. It not only starts our days off with fatigue and anxiety, but it can also rob us of peaceful nights. Simply asking God's forgiveness of the day's sins can give us that sense of newness—the assurance that tomorrow is indeed a new day and that we are unencumbered by the baggage of the past. That knowledge alone can enable our spirits, as well as our bodies, to rest.

At the end of even the most exhausting, exasperating, trying day, we can rest easy:

"I will praise the LORD, who counsels me; even at night my heart instructs me" (Psalm 16:7).

PRAYER

Dear Lord, thank You for the many ways You make it possible for me to feel at peace. I can end my days with my spirit truly at rest because of Your loving concern, Your unfailing forgiveness, Your constant guidance, and Your infinite graciousness. How blessed I am to be Your child. Amen.

SEVENTEEN

It's About Time

Teach us to number our days aright,
that we may gain a heart of wisdom.

Psalm 90:12

LET'S SLOW DOWN TODAY TO...

❧ *analyze how we spend our time;*

❧ *check whether the way we use our time truly reflects our priorities.*

Sherry walked into the meeting room carrying an assortment of papers and file folders, along with a thick, spiral-bound book.

"It's part of a new personal time-management system," she said, indicating the book, and proceeded to show it to me. It had a page for each day, with spaces to categorize the day's tasks as top priority, lesser priority, and "if I have time." The book had a section for yearly goals, monthly goals, weekly goals, and daily goals, as well as spaces for telephone numbers and addresses. There was even a place to schedule extracurricular activities. It was all very impressive.

"It's a great system," Sherry said pointedly. "You should try it."

She was probably right. Heaven knows I could use some help in managing my time.

How about you? Do you often come to the end of your work day and wonder how you could have worked for eight hours and accomplished so little? Or do you get up on Saturday morning, firmly committed to cleaning out the hall closet by noon, only to realize at 4:00 p.m. that you've worked on a dozen other things, but not that closet?

The topic of time management has certainly become a popular one in recent years, both in the corporate world and on the domestic front. God's desire is for us to use our time well, but to manage it according to His standards rather than those of the world.

The hours and days of our lives are a gift from God, and the way we use them is an exercise in stewardship of His blessings. As we get caught up in the trend to seek more effective use of our time, perhaps we need to ask ourselves what goals we have in doing so.

What do *you* want to accomplish in the time allotted to you for today? What about this week? This month? This year? Your life? What do you think God would have you do with the time He has given you? In keeping with that, how would you rank these tasks in terms of their priority in your life?

___ Going to work
___ Cleaning the hall closet
___ Working on the church bazaar
___ Having friends over for pizza
___ Relaxing with a book
___ Cooking
___ Attending your son's piano recital
___ Helping your daughter with her homework
___ Calling a friend whose father just died
___ Participating in a Bible study
___ Going to a movie

Add to the list all the other tasks and activities you might do in a typical week. All these things take time, and there simply isn't enough time to do all of them. How do you choose where to invest your time? It isn't easy, is it?

Imagine that you're starting a new job. The boss brings in a stack of computer printouts and says, "You have until 2:00 p.m. to finish these" and walks away without telling you what you are supposed to do with them. You may be the most efficient worker in the world; but if you don't know what you're supposed to do, you won't be able to complete the work.

Paul wrote to the Ephesians, "Therefore do not be foolish, but understand what the Lord's will is" (Ephesians 5:17). Even if you and I never had to go to our jobs, never had to maintain a household, never had to attend to the needs of our families, we still would not be able to accomplish God's will or carry out His work if we don't know what His will and His work are. We cannot manage our precious, God-given resource of time effectively until we set some fundamental priorities.

According to Jesus, God desires two basic things from us above all else: to love and serve Him and to care for our neighbors' needs (Matthew 22:37-40). The effective management of our time begins with those basic commitments. Once those are firmly in place, we can begin to sort out the tasks before us and to build the rich and joyful lifestyle He wants for us.

One of the most burdensome sources of stress in our lives is the feeling that we are spending our time on things that don't matter, that what we do is meaningless and without value. Investing our hours and our days according to God's commandments and

Christ's example ensures that our time will be used in ways that do matter — whether it's relaxing with a book to refresh our spirits, putting in another day on the job, or working day and night to renovate a center for the homeless.

For the Christian, time management isn't about completing more paperwork or getting the garage cleaned by Christmas. It's about letting God's commandments of love and service guide our decision-making; and it's about cherishing the precious resource of time He has given us.

PRAYER

God, thank You for giving me the hours and days of my life. Show me how You would have me use them to Your glory, that I might be a wise steward of Your gift of time. Amen.

PART THREE

ON-THE-JOB TRAINING

EIGHTEEN

Playing by the Rules

*Observe the commands of the LORD your God,
walking in his ways and revering him.*

Deuteronomy 8:6

LET'S SLOW DOWN TODAY TO...

❧ *think about the rules that prevail in the workplace;*

❧ *explore how God's rules apply on the job.*

Every workplace has its rules. Do any of these sound familiar?

- Please wash hands before returning to work.
- Smoking permitted in designated areas only.
- Persons entering this area must wear hard hats.
- Use fire door only in case of emergency.
- Do not turn thermostat below 68 degrees.
- All purchase orders must have supervisor's signature.

■ Please refill coffee pot if you take the last cup.
■ Loading Zone: No parking between 8:00 a.m. and 5:00 p.m.

The workplace seems to have rules everywhere we turn: tacked on the bulletin board, published in the employee handbook, printed on purchase order forms, taped to the copy machine, posted in the break room, and lettered on the wall in work areas. Those are just the official rules, of course. In addition, every work environment has its unofficial and unwritten rules:

■ If you go to a lunch meeting with Sue, don't order fish; she can't stand the smell of it.
■ Always answer the boss's phone, even if he's sitting right beside it.
■ Don't wear high heels that make you taller than the boss.
■ Clean up your desk before you go home so the department looks neat.
■ Never ask for time off during the busy season.

Since the workplace has its own sets of rules, both written and unwritten, where do God's rules—His commandments and His instructions for the way we are to live—fit in? Do we set them aside when we leave for work, and pick them up again when we come home?

Interestingly enough, much of what is considered sound management theory in today's corporate world is actually just a restatement of biblical principles. For example, the prophet Micah asked the rhetorical question, "And what does the LORD require of you? To act justly and to love mercy and to walk humbly with your God" (Micah 6:8). Translated into our on-the-job situation, this simply means that we are to deal fairly with others, to be patient and forgiving, and to demonstrate humility.

Certainly those qualities would be beneficial in any work setting, and would make bosses and subordinates alike easier to work with. With all the emphasis in today's workplace on team-building, cooperation, and employee satisfaction, fostering these qualities would surely go a long way toward creating a better corporate environment.

Here's another biblical rule that is especially useful in the workplace: "Everyone should be quick to listen, slow to speak and slow to become angry" (James 1:19). What changes would you see in your job environment if suddenly everyone in your workplace—including yourself—obeyed this rule? People making work assignments might not have to repeat their instructions as often, because their subordinates would have listened more carefully in the first place. Fewer mistakes and misunderstandings would arise. Fewer thoughtless or unkind remarks would get made, because people would start to think more carefully before they spoke. And instead of flying off the handle when conflict or pressure reached the boiling point, people would be "slow to anger," taking some time to cool off and look at the problem rationally.

One other biblical passage that would be a real asset in every workplace is this one: "Do not repay anyone evil for evil. Be careful to do what is right in the eyes of everybody. If it is possible, as far as it depends on you, live at peace with everyone" (Romans 12:17-18). Take a moment to think about the impact the principles of that passage could have in your workplace. Pretty staggering, isn't it? If we could only incorporate the Bible's rules into every employee handbook, every rules-and-regulations poster, and every operator's manual, today's workplace would experience a total revolution!

God's rules were created long before the first corporation was established, long before this age of computers and corporate relations and workplace psychology. Yet they are as pertinent and as beneficial in today's largest multinational company as they were among the wandering tribes of Israelites and the fledgling Christian communities of Bible times. What can you do this week to help make God's rules more a part of your workplace?

PRAYER

God, Your wisdom is overwhelming. In this era of laser communications and satellite technology and a worldwide marketplace, Your age-old guidelines for human social behavior are as timely as the newest computer chip. May I never lose sight of the perfection of Your rules for my day-to-day living. Amen.

NINETEEN

Comparison Shopping

Each one should test his own actions.
Then he can take pride in himself,
without comparing himself to somebody else,
for each one should carry his own load.

Galatians 6:4-5

❧ *consider why we so often compare ourselves to others and try to break the habit;*

❧ *learn to appreciate our own uniqueness.*

After her children grew up, Jenny went back to college to learn to be a court reporter. She worked hard on every assignment, almost never missed a class, and took a great deal of pride in the excellent grades she earned. She was excited about this new phase of her life.

One day, one of Jenny's teachers noticed that she seemed downcast, not at all her usual enthusiastic, outgoing self. After class, he asked her what was the matter.

"I'm wondering if I'm out of step," she answered.

"What do you mean?" he asked.

"Well," Jenny explained, "I was looking around the classroom today, and I noticed that about half the class isn't here. I know a lot of people cut class pretty much any time they feel like it. After all, they can still get by and graduate without coming to every class.

"And sometimes," she went on, "when I'm talking with the other students, I feel like I'm the only one who takes my work seriously. I know that's not the case; there are lots of others who are working just as hard as I am. But I feel like I'm in the minority. I guess it makes me wonder if I'm crazy to be putting so much effort into this program when I could get by with a lot less. It just makes me feel out of step."

"Jenny," the teacher said, "why did you enter this program in the first place?"

"Because I want to be able to get a job that pays well, but also because I wanted a challenge and a chance to develop a side of me that didn't get much attention while the kids were growing up."

"And are you getting what you came for?" he asked her.

"Absolutely! Coming back to school has been the best thing I could possibly have done for myself."

"Then does it really matter what any of the other students do or don't do?"

Jenny smiled.

"I guess not," she said. "I guess I need

to quit looking around the room and focus on my own goals, don't I?"

■

Jenny learned a vital lesson about comparison thinking. Being a comparison shopper can save us money at the supermarket, but getting into the habit of comparison thinking in relation to other people only causes us unhappiness. Yet the world fosters a constantly comparing mindset, and the workplace is an especially fertile field for making comparisons everywhere we turn.

In one of the first jobs I had after graduating from college, I made what I thought was an excellent salary. Everything was fine until one day I happened to learn that Joanne, another woman who had the same job as mine, was making significantly more, even though our backgrounds and experience were comparable.

I was so bothered by the situation that I asked my boss about it. He said, "Well, she just negotiated harder when we hired her than you did when we hired you."

That didn't make me feel any better. I let comparison thinking spoil both my enjoyment of my job *and* my relationship with Joanne. If only someone like Jenny's teacher had set my thinking straight!

Comparison thinking has a variety of negative effects.

Comparison thinking redirects our focus to human standards instead of divine standards. When we strive to adapt to the standards of those around us—whether they're higher standards or lower standards—then we compromise God's standards. We start to care more about measuring up to or fitting in with others than about pleasing Him. Since our accountability is ultimately to Him, we should look to Him for our comparisons: "So then, each of us will give an account of himself to God" (Romans 14:12).

Comparison thinking also jeopardizes relationships. Constantly comparing ourselves to others makes it impossible for us to view them with the love and acceptance that Christ's example teaches us. We're always evaluating them, seeing if they're measuring up to our standards or if we're measuring up to theirs. That's no basis for a sincere, genuinely caring relationship.

Comparison thinking leads to jealousy. The Bible cites jealousy as one of the most undesirable and destructive qualities of human nature. Jealousy gets its foothold when we start comparing ourselves to others.

Letting the green-eyed monster take up residence in our lives through comparison thinking is a real threat to our spiritual well-being and our day-to-day happiness.

PRAYER

God, free me from comparison thinking. Being the person You want me to be is a full-time job. Help me to keep my comparisons focused on Your Word and Your work in my life. Amen.

TWENTY

Ol' Green Eyes

A heart at peace gives life to the body,
but envy rots the bones.

Proverbs 14:30

🙠 *practice positive steps to keep jealousy from being a part of our lives;*

🙠 *be alert to conditions that lead to jealousy.*

This is an exercise. In the first column of spaces below, list the names of five people you know who possess something you wish you had. It can be a personal quality, a talent, a job, a relationship, or another life circumstance. In the space opposite each name, write down what they have that you would like to have.

1. _____   _____

2. _____   _____

3. _____   _____

4. _____   _____

5. _____   _____

All of us could probably come up with a much longer list than the one above. I can find numerous I-wish-I-hads just by thinking about my friends: Cathy's athletic ability, Dawn's spiritual maturity, Lynn's talent for organization.

One of the most splendid mysteries of God's plan is that He made each of us different and gave each of us a different set of raw materials and circumstances through which to do His work. Unfortunately, because we are human and don't always reflect a Christlike spirit, these differences can often lead to what the Bible calls jealousy or envy.

Both the Old and New Testaments warn us clearly and repeatedly about the perils of a jealous spirit. Job 5:2 says, "Resentment kills a fool, and envy slays the simple." Jesus included envy in a list of evils that come from within us and make us "unclean": evil thoughts, sexual immorality, theft, murder, adultery, greed, malice, deceit, lewdness, envy, slander, arrogance, and folly (Mark 7:21-22). Paul, too, in his letter to the Galatians, lumps both envy and jealousy in with a list of ugly "acts of the sinful nature" (Galatians 5:20-21). He also tells the Corinthians that they are still worldly "since there is jealousy and quarreling among

[them]" (1 Corinthians 3:3).

According to the dictionary, envy arises when we see that someone else has something we want; as a result, we feel discontented with our own lot and resentful toward that other person. Jealousy has these same components, with the added element of fear: we fear that the other person will be loved or admired or appreciated or rewarded more than we are.

Being constantly dissatisfied with ourselves and our lives, harboring ill feelings toward others, and always being afraid that someone will outshine us is a painful way to live. It's not surprising that God wants us to be free from jealousy's grip. An envious spirit blocks us from living the rich and joyful lives He desires for us.

What should we do, then, when those twinges—or yanks—of jealousy threaten to take hold of us?

First, we need simply to recognize them for what they are: the reactions of the worldly nature to seeing that someone else has something we want. If we are alert to the stirrings of jealousy, we can deal with them before they start to color our outlook. When we recognize the beginnings of envy and jealousy, we can choose not to give them a foothold, and then turn to the Holy Spirit for the strength to follow through.

Second, we can turn our envy into a motivation for positive change. For example, I would love to have my friend Peggy's sparkling, gracious personality that seems to draw people to her like a magnet. She is unquestionably the most instantly likable person I have ever met.

I'm pretty sure no one is going to give me a gift-wrapped package containing a personality makeover; so, instead of letting myself be devoured by envy over Peggy's personality, I've made it my goal to learn as much as I can from her. I try to identify the qualities that make her so likable and imitate them in my own day-to-day interactions.

I try to maintain the same attitude toward Donna, a coworker who walks into the office every day looking like a fashion model. It isn't that she dresses expensively, because I know she doesn't spend a lot on her clothes. But she has style. One day I decided to start observing carefully how she put her outfits together, to see what I could learn. Sometimes I even asked her for ideas about my own wardrobe, and she was always happy to help me. It made her feel good to know that I admired her taste, and learning from her was a lot more fun than sitting back and feeling envious.

Look back at the list you made at the beginning of this chapter. What can you learn from each person you listed?

Sometimes, though, we feel jealous when other people seem to have all the luck. They have the best jobs, the nicest houses, the happiest marriages, or the biggest incomes. We feel a sense of injustice that they have things we don't have. We feel as though no matter how much we apply ourselves or strive to do our best, we'll never have what they have.

We all need to learn more about how to deal with this kind of jealousy.

PRAYER

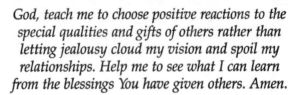

God, teach me to choose positive reactions to the special qualities and gifts of others rather than letting jealousy cloud my vision and spoil my relationships. Help me to see what I can learn from the blessings You have given others. Amen.

TWENTY-ONE

I Just Want My Share

Yet you say, "The way of the Lord is not just."
Hear, O house of Israel: Is my way unjust?
Is it not your ways that are unjust?

Ezekiel 18:25

Ron is a coworker of mine who has many years of experience in corporate personnel work and human resources management. One day when we were talking about the personnel problems that large organizations have, he said, "Jealousy is a tremendous problem in almost every organization." Much to my chagrin, he went on to say that the problem is generally much worse where there is a high percentage of women employees.

I hated hearing him say that, partly because I suspected it was true and partly because I have always believed so strongly in equality in the workplace. I don't like to think that women cause problems in a work setting any more than men do.

Whether we like it or not, though, jealousy is a problem in the workplace. It interferes with our Christian witness by making us think, say, and do unChristlike things. It spoils our relationships with others and can taint our entire attitude about our jobs and our coworkers.

We have looked at some ways to deal with those petty jealousies that we encounter day-to-day, like envy of someone else's appearance or personality. But what about a more powerful, consuming jealousy, not of some quality or small possession, but of a person's whole lifestyle?

As an example, let's say the company that you and I work for has just hired Rita to be the new vice-president. She's tall, thin and attractive; she has a big, fancy office, gets invited to all the important business and social functions, and — according to rumor — makes a salary that boggles the mind. Even the car she drives exudes glamour and success. Every time we pass her in the hallway, our self-esteem drops to the basement. Seeing someone like Rita, who seems to have everything we want, makes us feel like we don't have anything! We're just plain jealous.

What principles does the Bible offer to

help us handle these unpleasant, worldly reactions?

We can place our complete trust in God's justice. As is often the case, our jealousy of Rita gives rise to the feeling that life just isn't fair. We are outraged that the distribution of the world's riches—whether money, talent, physical attributes, relationships, or anything else—should be so inequitable. We can't stand the idea that someone else got a bigger piece of the pie than we did.

We cannot overcome jealousy until we learn to trust God's standard of justice instead of the world's. Wanting life to be fair, as we understand it, is a human notion. If you give candy to a group of children, it's only fair to divide the candy equally, right? But God's universe doesn't operate on the same principles as giving children candy, and we will only frustrate ourselves if we try to force Him into our understanding. "'For my thoughts are not your thoughts, neither are your ways my ways,' declares the LORD. 'As the heavens are higher than the earth, so are my ways higher than your ways'" (Isaiah 55:8-9).

God's plan is beyond our understanding, but total justice undergirds it. "The LORD is known by his justice" (Psalm 9:16).

The world's best is nothing compared to

God's best for us. We want what the world can give us. We look at people around us who have what we want, and we convince ourselves that having what they have would be best for us. Yet we don't know what those people may have lost or sacrificed or endured as the price of what they have. Only God has the eternal perspective and the perfect vision to see what is best for us. Once again, trust is at the core.

When we let ourselves be consumed by jealousy, it reflects a lack of trust in God to care for us. God calls us to look at things from a different perspective: "And we know that in all things God works for the good of those who love him, who have been called according to his purpose" (Romans 8:28).

Overcoming jealousy is an act of spiritual discipline. When we choose to seek God's help in overcoming jealousy instead of letting it put a lock on our spirits, we are exercising spiritual discipline. In doing so, we give God's will priority over our own — as His Word instructs us to do. Spiritual discipline consists of choosing His ways over the world's. At the same time, we are choosing to draw on the resources of the Holy Spirit instead of being victimized by negative human emotions.

In short, when we overcome jealousy we

are flexing our spiritual muscles, helping to train ourselves and grow in strength for the next spiritual challenge that lies ahead. Beginning to conquer jealousy is both a major victory in our quest for more Christlike living and a big step toward more joyful and peaceful workdays.

PRAYER

God, give me a trusting heart. Teach me to rely on Your ultimate justice and to trust in Your graciousness. Fill me so completely with the riches of Your Spirit that I have no need to envy what others have been given. Amen.

TWENTY-TWO

A Troublemaker? *Moi?*

*Blessed are the peacemakers,
for they will be called sons of God.*

Matthew 5:9

≥● *commit to being a peacemaker in our work setting;*

≥● *make efforts to reduce conflict between others rather than foster it.*

Gail and Patricia worked together for three years as computer programmers for the same company. When the position of Senior Programmer became available, they both applied for it.

Patricia was chosen for the promotion. Gail sent her a potted plant for her new office, along with a card that said, "Congratulations. I know you'll do a great job."

About a month later, Gail was chatting with another programmer, Linda, in the break room.

"So how do you think Pat is doing as Senior Programmer?" Linda asked her.

"I think she's doing a great job. I knew she would," Gail replied.

"I hear that some of the people over in New Product Development don't like the new procedures she's come up with," Linda said.

"Well, changes are always hard for people to adapt to. I know Pat gives everything a lot of thought before she makes decisions. The way she's approaching the job might not be the same way you or I or the guys in New Products would do it, but Pat's a good programmer and I just hope everyone gives her a chance to prove herself."

"I guess so. Well, I'd better get back to work."

A few days later, Linda ran into Patricia in the hallway.

"So how's the new job going?" Linda asked.

"Oh, pretty well. You know how it is with a new job—you feel like you have to learn so much so fast that your brain will burst!"

"Gail seems to feel pretty bad about not getting the job; how do you think she's handling it?"

"Handling it? Well, she and I really are good friends; I think she's genuinely happy for me."

"I just wondered, because she mentioned that if she had gotten the job, she would probably have approached things differently than you are. She seems to think you're trying really hard to prove yourself."

"What does that mean? Doesn't she like the way I'm doing the job? I can't believe she would say that behind my back. I can't help it if the vice-president thought that I was better qualified for the job than she was. I certainly don't want it to get in the way of our friendship."

The next day, Linda ran into Gail again.

"I was talking to Patricia the other day. She seems to think you might be a little jealous about not getting the job."

"What?" Gail said, surprised. "What would make her think that?"

"Well, I don't know," Linda answered. "She kind of sounded like she thought you couldn't accept the fact that she was better qualified for the job."

"Better qualified? Our backgrounds are almost identical. I can't believe she would say that. She knows I'm just as good a programmer as she is. Maybe this job has changed her. Or maybe she's just not as good a friend as I thought."

■

Apparently, Linda wasn't familiar with the verse in Proverbs that says, "A perverse man stirs up dissension, and a gossip separates close friends" (16:28). She was simply being perverse. Gail and Patricia's friendship wasn't affected by Patricia's promotion—until Linda got involved. Linda may not even have meant to, but she was constantly stirring up trouble between the other two women.

Let's see what we can learn from her about office peacemaking.

Exercise judgment in what you repeat. There was no beneficial reason for Linda to repeat the rumored complaints from the people in New Products. Before we repeat something we've heard, it's wise to screen it with the following questions:

Is there a good reason to repeat this?

What might the consequences be if I repeat this?

Do I know that what I'm repeating is true?

Don't distort what people say and then repeat it as though it were fact. Gail never said she didn't like the way Patricia was doing the job, but Linda let Patricia think she had said so. In fact, from person to person, Linda continued to distort what was actually said.

Don't speculate out loud about what somebody else thinks or feels. Linda was really only speculating about Gail's feelings of jealousy; Gail never expressed any. Her speculation was an unfair appraisal and misrepresented the truth.

Learn to be comfortable in not saying anything. The Bible tells us to be "slow to speak" (James 1:19) and to practice judicious silence. Our environment bombards us so constantly with communication that silence often makes us uncomfortable. Learning to practice silence, though, can save us a great deal of stress and misunderstanding in our day-to-day lives. And silence may well be one of our best tools, as we seek to become the peacemakers God calls us to be.

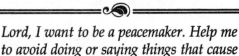

PRAYER

Lord, I want to be a peacemaker. Help me to avoid doing or saying things that cause dissension among others. Give me the wisdom and insight to discern what actions I can take that will truly bring peace into the workplace and the world around me. Amen.

TWENTY-THREE

Am I Cracking Up?

Brothers, do not slander one another.

James 4:11

I used to have an office with a big picture window along one wall. As is common in Florida, the window was coated with clear, dark-tinted film to keep the afternoon sun from heating up the room.

One day, when I was doing paperwork at my desk, I heard a *pop*, like a shot from a toy gun. It came from the side of the room where the window was. Looking up, I watched the most bizarre thing happen. A small crack had appeared in the center of the window. Within seconds, the crack branched into more and more cracks until the entire window was broken into tiny pieces. The only reason it didn't collapse into a heap of crystalline fragments was that the solar film was holding the pieces together.

I immediately called the maintenance supervisor, who came up to take a look. He looked at the window from the inside and the outside, scratched his head for a while, and finally said, "The only thing I can think of is that the glass got too warm, and then suddenly cooled off. It contracted too fast, and just broke.

"You know," he went on, "if it hadn't been for that solar film holding that thing together, you could have been showered with flying glass. You were lucky."

■

I can still picture that window breaking. In my mind's eye I can see that tiny crack branching, spreading, multiplying until the whole window was destroyed. It's a dramatic illustration of how a tiny bit of damage can produce total destruction as quickly as the blink of an eye.

The tiny crack that resulted in a shattered window is an accurate illustration of how office gossip works, too. When I hear someone—including myself—begin to gossip, I think of that window. A slanderous or catty or unkind remark is like that first tiny crack where the damage begins. The crack spreads when someone who hears that remark repeats it to someone else, and then that person repeats it, and before long, something has been broken into pieces: a person's reputation, a friendship, a coworker's chances for promotion, someone else's sense of self-worth or well-being.

Every work environment with more than a handful of employees has its grapevine, its unofficial communication network that's fed by the rumor mill and sustained by jealousy, pettiness, vindictiveness, and a whole host of other unpleasant human qualities. Gossip is an accepted fact of corporate life and has become the workplace equivalent of the Great American Pastime.

Are these situations familiar?

Jeanine comes back from a two-week vacation and asks her coworkers eagerly, "So—what did I miss? Fill me in!"

Teresa goes out to lunch with her friend Sue, who works in another department and asks, "Well, what's the latest news about Pam's fights with her husband?"

The sales department clerks all go to lunch together and the first topic of conversation is the boss's new secretary. "Why did he hire her?" "She seems pretty sold on herself, if you ask me." "I think her outfit is a little on the racy side for the office."

We all do it. We're interested in others' lives and in what goes on around us. We like to be in the know. And we all like to express our opinions.

Gossip can start out as innocently as just an exchange of news and views—what we did over the weekend, how we like the newest movie, our kids' latest escapades. Before long, though, the conversation deteriorates into Let's-pick-apart-the-boss or Can-you-believe-she-did-that?

Gossip—along with its close and ugly companion, slander—may be a fact of workplace life, but it's certainly not biblical: "Whoever spreads slander is a fool" (Proverbs 10:18); "And not only do they become idlers, but also gossips and busybodies, saying things they ought not to" (1 Timothy 5:13); "But now you must rid yourselves of all such things as these: anger, rage, malice, slander" (Colossians 3:8).

According to the Bible, then, gossips cannot be trusted. They betray confidences, come between friends, and destroy their own relationships as well; they speak foolishly, without weighing the consequences of their words, and speculate on things that don't concern them.

Alone, we cannot conquer the human tendency that leads us to speak unkindly or untruthfully or thoughtlessly about others. It's too much a part of us, especially in the work environment where there is so much encouragement to gossip. But with the restraining, guiding help of the Holy Spirit and a personal commitment to more godly speaking, we can change our habits.

We can make the difference between a tiny crack and a shattered window in another person's life.

PRAYER

*Lord, help me to remember the hurt and
the destruction that gossip can cause. Give me
the self-control to avoid participating
in the office grapevine and to conquer
the petty jealousies that feed unkind remarks
and useless speculation. Let me be
a positive force for change. Amen.*

TWENTY-FOUR

Cross My Heart

*No one who practices deceit will dwell
in my house; no one who speaks falsely
will stand in my presence.*

Psalm 101:7

LET'S SLOW DOWN TODAY TO...

≥▲ *be alert to small deceptions that may creep into our daily living;*

≥▲ *choose not to participate in deceit, even though it may be accepted in the workplace.*

Louise is having a job interview. As Mr. Anderson begins to question her, she wonders just how much she should tell him.

Mr. Anderson tells her, "What we're really looking for in this position is some-one who's interested in the future and a long-term relationship with our company. I see that you've been out of the workplace for a few years. What prompted you to job-hunt now?"

Louise thinks to herself, *I don't have much choice: I have to get a job to help with expenses for a year until my husband finishes his computer training course. Then I can go back to staying at home with the kids like I want to.*

But to Mr. Anderson she replies, "Well, even though I've been staying at home for the past few years, the children are older now, and I'm ready to get back into the job market and really start to build a career for myself. Your company sounds like just what I'm looking for."

Susan, the head of the research department, is panicking because a major report is due tomorrow and the work isn't done. She desperately needs Rod, her assistant, to stay late tonight and help her wrap up the report. She thinks to herself, *Rod isn't going to like this. He's been really overworked these last several weeks already, and it's not going to let up, either. There's another big project waiting in the wings as soon as this one's finished — but he doesn't know that.*

She says to Rod, "I really need you to help me wrap up this report tonight. After it's done, things are going to lighten up a lot in the department and maybe you can get some time off, okay?"

Elaine's boss, Claire, is furious. A shipment of important patient record forms for the hospital where they work has just been delivered, and they're the wrong ones. Elaine realizes she made a mistake when she placed the order, but she tells Claire:

"I don't know what's wrong with our supplier these days. I heard that the accounting department has had trouble with them, too. They obviously just shipped the wrong forms. I'll call them and find out what their problem is."

■

Neither Louise nor Susan nor Elaine has done anything that hasn't been done before. Louise is misrepresenting her career plans in order to land a job she needs. Susan is misleading Rod about the upcoming workload so she can meet her deadline. And Elaine is placing the blame on someone else for a mistake she made.

We can call it playing the corporate game and excuse it by saying "Everybody does it." But according to the Bible, Louise, Susan, and Elaine are all doing something else: They're practicing deceit and being dishonest. To meet their own ends, they're causing another person to believe something that isn't true. Mr. Anderson thinks Louise is ready to launch a career with the company, when that isn't what she wants at all. Susan is promising Rod some time off, which he isn't going to get. Claire is convinced that her supplier of medical forms is unreliable, which isn't true.

■

Ask any one of these same people the following question: "If one of your children lied, would you punish him?" They'll answer emphatically, "Of course! I'm teaching my children the importance of telling the truth!" Yet each of them is willing to lie and deceive others in the workplace.

The Bible specifically cautions us against several kinds of deceit, including:

> ■ *Accusing others falsely*—"You shall not give false testimony against your neighbor." (Exodus 20:16)
> ■ *Insincerity*—"Do not drag me away with the wicked, with those who do evil, who speak cordially with their neighborsbut harbor malice in their hearts." (Psalm 28:3)
> ■ *Slandering others behind their backs*— "Whoever slanders his neighbor in secret, him will I put to silence." (Psalm 101:5)
> ■ *Lying*—"Therefore each of you must put off falsehood and speak truthfully to his neighbor." (Ephesians 4:25)

Practicing deceit may be part of the corporate game — but the Bible tells us we're not to play.

TWENTY-FIVE

Staying in Shape

Do you not know that in a race all the runners run, but only one gets the prize? Run in such a way as to get the prize. Everyone who competes in the games goes into strict training. They do it to get a crown that will not last; but we do it to get a crown that will last forever.

1 Corinthians 9:24-25

❧ *consider the need for spiritual exercise;*

❧ *identify ways to cultivate spiritual maturity through training and practice.*

Suzanne is a walking advertisement for aerobics training. She has a trim, well-proportioned figure and exudes energy and vitality. Three nights a week, you can see her at her aerobics class, stretching and reaching and kicking to the music. She actually looks like she enjoys it, too!

The importance of exercise to good physical health has certainly moved to the forefront of our attention in recent years. But what about good spiritual health? Is it important to exercise our spiritual selves in order to stay in peak condition?

The apostle Paul seemed to think so. He compared the Christian life to a race, in which the prize is eternal life in God's

Kingdom: "Forgetting what is behind . . . I press on toward the goal . . . to win the prize for which God has called me heavenward in Christ Jesus" (Philippians 3:13-14). If we are to run the race successfully, he says, we must go into strict training (1 Corinthians 9:25).

What does spiritual training involve?

Stretching. Almost any exercise program involves stretching to increase the flexibility and reach of our muscles. We stretch spiritually when we ask more of ourselves today than we did yesterday; when we exert ourselves to pray more faithfully, to reach out to others more actively, to exercise compassion or self-control or patience more consistently. We also stretch when we rely on the Holy Spirit more frequently to empower us to do things we cannot do by ourselves, instead of struggling along in frustration with our own limitations. What areas of your spiritual life need a little stretching?

Toning. An aerobics teacher at the local recreation center recently described for me what toning is. "It's sculpting your body," she explained. "It's giving your muscles definition—'tone.' Exercises used for toning don't involve big, sweeping movements or fast repetitions; they require discipline and control."

Toning our spiritual selves involves

cultivating inner discipline and developing a Christlike attitude of mind and heart. It includes learning to view the world around us more through God's eyes than human eyes and maintaining an eternal perspective in a world that is so insistently demanding attention to the here and now. Spiritual toning is the result of study, reflection, and careful attention to God's presence and work in our lives. Our spirits require discipline and control.

Endurance. You can always spot the new students in an aerobics class: they're the ones who are puffing and panting the most! Gradually, though, we build up our endurance. As the days and weeks go by, we find we can do more sit-ups or jog in place longer or get through more routines without resting. But it takes time. It also takes commitment, consistency, and follow-through.

Building spiritual endurance requires the same things. We cannot expect to have the strength and spiritual maturity to endure life's most painful and demanding experiences if we don't build that endurance over time. We build endurance for life's crises by demanding more and more of ourselves in the day-to-day business of living for Christ — and by accepting more and more of His help as we go. "If we endure, we will also reign with him" (2 Timothy 2:12).

Practice. Whether it's playing the piano or typing or managing computer data or performing aerobics routines, we cannot do most things well without practice. Think about the aspects of your job that you do effortlessly and confidently, simply because you've had so much practice at doing them.

Effective Christian living requires practice, too. For example, Paul told us that "the fruit of the Spirit is love, joy, peace, patience, kindness, goodness, faithfulness, gentleness and self-control" (Galatians 5:22). How can we cultivate these qualities of the Spirit if we don't *practice* them? The workplace is an ideal setting for practicing our Christian living. Where better to learn how to put love into action, to reflect the joy of Christ's presence, to be a peacemaker, to exercise patience, to do kindnesses for others, to discern good from evil, to demonstrate faithfulness, to be gentle, and to practice self-control?

Spiritual fitness, like physical fitness, comes from stretching, toning, endurance, and practice. Unlike physical exercise, though, we have unlimited resources on which to draw as we work through our training program. How about launching a fitness plan for yourself this week?

PRAYER

Lord, I know I cannot sit back and expect spiritual maturity to come to me, any more than I can expect physical fitness to simply happen without hard work and commitment. Help me to train myself to run my race "in such a way as to get the prize." Amen.

TWENTY-SIX

The Dog Ate My Homework

For since the creation of the world God's
invisible qualities — his eternal power
and divine nature — have been clearly seen,
being understood from what has been made,
so that men are without excuse.

Romans 1:20

LET'S SLOW DOWN TODAY TO...

✎ *explore why we make excuses for the things we do or fail to do;*

✎ *change our excuse-making behavior.*

What is it that makes us need to find excuses for the things we do that we shouldn't, or the things we fail to do that we should?

We seem to learn this habit as children. How many times, between the ages of four and eighteen do you suppose you told your parents, teachers, or other adults:

"I forgot."

"I didn't hear you."

"I didn't think you meant today."

Unfortunately, this pattern of excuse-making seems to follow most of us into the workplace. The only difference is that we get a little more sophisticated and creative with our excuses.

Boss: The minutes of the board meeting were supposed to be mailed out yesterday, and I haven't even seen the first draft. Where are they?

Employee: I took my notes from the meeting home to work on, and my son picked them up by mistake and accidentally turned them in to his science teacher in place of his report on "Why Old Bananas Turn Brown."

We find it so hard to say, "I made a mistake," or "I didn't follow through as I should have," or "I misunderstood what you wanted me to do." Instead, we feel we have to find some way to rationalize our errors, our misunderstandings, and our lack of attention to our responsibilities.

We use this same approach when we try to explain away our failure to live as God wants us to. The same excuses that came so easily to us as children creep into our spiritual lives.

"I forgot." Sometimes we simply forget to consider God's desires and His commandments in any given situation. Or maybe we make a decision—consciously or unconsciously—to neglect His desires in favor

of some other human need. Then we tell ourselves we "forgot." We forgot to be patient or compassionate when a coworker was having a difficult time. We forgot to be forgiving when a friend's thoughtless behavior made us angry. We forgot God's standards of morality when an attractive man made a suggestive invitation.

Remembering God's commandments isn't an option. His Word isn't like a lunch appointment or a project deadline, to be remembered or forgotten depending on what else is occupying our minds at the time. His sovereignty over our lives and His desire for us to live according to His will is to be at the very core of everything we are and do.

"*I didn't hear you.*" Our lives are filled with noise. Where I work, it's the click and beep of computer terminals, the whine of laser printers, the chiming of telephones, and the conversations of busy, energetic people hard at work. At home, it's the voices from television sitcoms and cartoons, the bleeps and pings of video games, the crashing bass music on a teenager's stereo, the ringing of the phone, the conversation of family members. No wonder we're tempted to tell God, "I didn't hear You."

We pray to God for guidance or insight or simply the strength to get through another day, and yet our lives become so cluttered with other noise that we can't hear His voice. Then we feel let down that He hasn't answered us.

When we find ourselves telling God, "I didn't hear You," we may not have made ourselves available to hear Him. We haven't attuned ourselves to what He might have to say to us. We haven't set aside quiet times for ourselves and Him. We haven't opened our hearts and minds with sensitivity to His leading. We haven't looked at what's going on around us with a mind to see His hand in it. No wonder we can't hear Him.

"I didn't know you meant today." Procrastination is one of the more common human tendencies. Whether at work or at home, we tend to put off doing things that might be difficult or time-consuming or maybe even distasteful.

We put off doing the things God wants us to do, too. We put off investing more time in prayer and study because it's inconvenient. We put off becoming more involved in our church because we're not sure where we fit into the program. We put off extending an act of friendship to a new coworker because we're afraid she might reject us.

We could well add the word *today* to every instruction God has given us in His

Word. When Christ told us to love and honor God and to love and serve others, He didn't add "when it's convenient for you." When He said, "Go and make disciples of all nations" (Matthew 28:19), He didn't tell us to pencil it in for 1998. His call to us is today, now, this minute.

No more excuses.

PRAYER

God, make me more alert to my own excuse-making. Help me to remember Your commandments in every situation, to hear Your voice amid all the noise of my life, and constantly to sense the urgency, the today-ness of Your commandments. May I live courageously and wholly for You. Amen.

TWENTY-SEVEN

Eyeball to Eyeball

"How can you say to your brother, 'Brother, let me take the speck out of your eye,' when you yourself fail to see the plank in your own eye? You hypocrite, first take the plank out of your eye, and then you will see clearly to remove the speck from your brother's eye."

Luke 6:42

LET'S SLOW DOWN TODAY TO...

ع‌ـ *learn to respect differences and value the uniqueness of those around us;*

ع‌ـ *adopt a balanced view of our own shortcomings.*

"Fred always turns the copier off when he's finished, so that the next person has to wait for it to warm up. He's so inconsiderate!"

"I wish Lois wouldn't constantly be touching up her makeup at her desk. She thinks this department is a beauty shop."

"I can't stand the tone of voice Mrs. Simms uses when she tells us about the latest new rules the management committee has come up with. She thinks she's Moses reporting the Ten Commandments."

Let's face it. Any time a group of people work together—even the nicest people in the world—they will, inevitably and innocently, do things from time to time that will drive each other absolutely nuts. One of the realities of the workplace is that we spend our on-the-job hours surrounded by people whose company we did not seek and whose acquaintance we did not choose. They are people whose values, political opinions, tastes, personalities, beliefs, work styles, and overall outlooks on life may be different from ours—slightly different, moderately different, or astronomically different.

We, as Christian women in the workplace, have a perfect opportunity to influence the way these differences are dealt with by those around us. We can, in effect, create an example for others in our workplace. What guidelines does the Bible give us for keeping our workplace free of "speckled" vision?

Acknowledge and accept each person's uniqueness and worth. Being different is part of God's design for human beings, and each unique individual is equally important to Him. Once we abandon our insistence that everyone think, act and be just like us, we can enjoy the vast diversity of human beings.

Take a balanced view of our own strengths and weaknesses. Paul's advice to us is clear: "Do not think of yourself more highly than you ought, but rather think of yourself with sober judgment, in accordance with the measure of faith God has given you" (Romans 12:3). All of us have our idiosyncracies. It is unlikely that ours are any more or any less glaring than others'. When we focus on removing the planks in our own eyes, we have a lot less time and energy to invest in worrying about the shortcomings and peculiarities of those around us.

Be a force for peace. Differences can cause divisiveness and conflict. They can be emphasized all out of proportion, generating a constant atmosphere of criticism and a state of chronic tension and conflict. Or, differences can provide a stimulating and challenging work environment. If we take seriously God's call to be peacemakers, we can have a major impact on how differences affect our work situation.

For example, when we hear a coworker moan about Fred's leaving the copier on, we might encourage her to mention it to him instead of criticizing him behind his back. He's probably just trying to reduce the company's electric bill anyway! And when someone complains about Mrs. Simms' delivery of the management committee commandments, we might say something like, "She just wants to be sure we understand the new policies."

What are the differences that cause you tension in your work area? Into which category do they fall? Are they (1) those that can be chalked up to human diversity and simply overlooked or tolerated; or (2) those that need to be dealt with in a positive, gentle, and practical way—perhaps by simply asking a question, initiating a constructive conversation, or making a helpful suggestion? What can you do this week to change how you are affected by these differences?

If differences trouble you, ask yourself this: Would I *really* want to work with a whole group of people exactly like me? I don't know about you, but my answer is "How boring!" I definitely like God's way better.

PRAYER

Lord, open my eyes to the richness of individual differences. Help me to address my own weaknesses instead of judging the weaknesses of others. Give me the same spirit of love and patience with others that You extend to me. Amen.

PART FOUR

EMPLOYEE BENEFITS

TWENTY-EIGHT

A Little Seasoning

*"Even the stork in the sky knows her
appointed seasons, and the dove,
the swift and the thrush observe the time
of their migration. But my people do not know
the requirements of the LORD."*

Jeremiah 8:7

❧ *consider the seasons of our lives;*

❧ *seek an understanding of God's seasons.*

I keep a list of the things I'm going to do when I'm retired and don't have to go to work. For example:

1. I am going to write thank-you notes to anyone and everyone who does anything nice for me, from the grocery cashier to the president of the telephone company.
2. I am going to act on my kind impulses, like "I should bake a casserole for Mrs. Fenser while she's sick," instead of deciding I'm too busy.
3. I am going to bring treats for the children every time I visit someone who has them.

4. I am going to send birthday cards by the dozen, never missing the birthday of a friend or relative.
5. I am never, ever, ever going to wear pantyhose.

What would your list look like? Take a moment to fantasize about the things you would like to do if you had more time. It's fun, isn't it?

The Bible tells us that "there is a time for everything, and a season for every activity under heaven" (Ecclesiastes 3:1). My list of things to do when I'm retired is founded on the premise that someday my life will enter a different season, one in which less of my time and energy will be devoted to my job and to the immediate needs of a busy family.

We sometimes cause ourselves unnecessary stress by disregarding this biblical concept of seasons. We try too hard to be "a woman for all seasons" at all times—probably because that's what our modern culture has convinced us we ought to be. We try to fulfill the roles of wife and mother in the same way our mothers might have, while at the same time fulfilling the equally demanding roles of breadwinners. Instead of identifying the current season of our lives and living accordingly, we try to live as though there were no seasons, as though we have to do it all now, have it all now, know it all now.

Seasons are part of God's design for His creation. Just as the dove, the swift, and the thrush know their appointed seasons, so we should know the seasons in our lives—the proper times to devote ourselves to particular activities.

Youth has its own season: "Be happy, young man, while you are young, and let your heart give you joy in the days of your youth" (Ecclesiastes 11:9). Parenthood, too, has its own season: "Train a child in the way he should go, and when he is old he will not turn from it" (Proverbs 22:6).

In fact, parenthood brings a heightened awareness of our lives as a series of seasons. When my son was a toddler, I longed for a time when my house would not be strewn with toys from wall to wall, and when I could come and go without diaper bag, bottle, snacks, and the other paraphernalia of babyhood. Now my house is neater and I've given away the diaper bag. Now a handsome, lanky teenager lives in my home, and we talk about the dilemmas of dating and drugs. A different season indeed.

Those of us who work outside the home—

as well as our at-home friends — tend to feel that our lives will always be like this: crammed with hectic, crowded, often frustrating and harrying days; filled with job concerns, career decisions, time pressures, and work/home conflicts; allowing little time for ourselves and the many other things we would like to do. Learning to recognize God's plan of seasons in our lives offers us a great measure of peace and serenity. It frees us from the pressure of having to do and be everything today. It gives us an affection for the past, an appreciation of the present, and a joyful anticipation of the future.

Reflect for a moment on the season your life is in now. What are its hallmarks? How will it change in five or ten years? How is it different from a decade ago, or five years ago? What do you treasure most about the past seasons? What do you anticipate most enthusiastically about future ones? Are there things you are trying to do or be right now that could be better incorporated into a future season — or maybe should be abandoned to the past?

As we reflect on the seasons in our lives, though, there's one vital aspect to remember: following Christ's example and carrying out God's work are never out of season. Our mission to serve Him is as urgent when our lives are busy and filled with earthly demands as it is when we have more leisure and less pressure. We cannot use God's gift of seasons as an excuse for putting off His work. As Paul admonished Timothy, "Preach the Word; be prepared in season and out of season" (2 Timothy 4:2).

God's work is not to wait until it's convenient or popular or easy. His season is now, just as it was yesterday and will be tomorrow. As our lives move through their many seasons, His loving presence and our devoted discipleship are the constants.

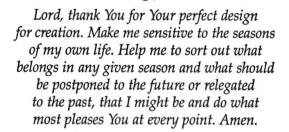

PRAYER

Lord, thank You for Your perfect design for creation. Make me sensitive to the seasons of my own life. Help me to sort out what belongs in any given season and what should be postponed to the future or relegated to the past, that I might be and do what most pleases You at every point. Amen.

TWENTY-NINE

What a Difference!

We are hard pressed on every side, but not crushed; perplexed, but not in despair; persecuted, but not abandoned; struck down, but not destroyed.

2 Corinthians 4:8-9

❧ *gather strength from the assurance that God cares and is in control;*

❧ *practice relying on Him instead of on ourselves.*

During their coffee break, Patricia and Marian were talking about their coworker, Virginia. All three women work for an accounting firm, and it's the height of income tax season.

Marian said, "When I think about all the problems Virginia has been through during the past year, I can't believe that she's even sane. First, her husband is diagnosed as having cancer. Then, her daughter gets arrested for possession of drugs. And on top of that, this is our busiest time of year at work and everybody's putting in tons of overtime. The job pressure alone is making me crazy. I just don't know how Virginia handles all those other things.

"And do you know, I haven't heard that woman complain once—about any of it? I think the closest thing to a complaint I've heard is when she said one day, 'I'm really tired this morning; my husband had a bad night.'"

■

Virginia would be surprised and flattered by her friends' praise. For her, the past several months have been a nightmare; there's no doubt about that. She's spent many nights crying, feeling overwhelmed by sheer physical and emotional fatigue.

If Marian and Patricia asked Virginia her "secret," she'd probably tell them this:

"When my husband and I were first told he had cancer, I felt the whole world crashing in on me. I thought, *How am I going to handle this?* It didn't take me long to realize that I couldn't—alone. I had to turn my life, and Don's life, over to God and commit us to His care. I knew my own strength wasn't enough for the strain of facing Don's illness. I had to rely on God.

"When my daughter's problems started to surface, I said, 'Lord, Karen is in Your hands. Guide me and strengthen me in deciding what I have to do. I'm just entrusting this whole family to You.'

"Sure, I still cry a lot and get worn out, and there are times I don't know what to do. But surprisingly enough, I never feel defeated; I never feel truly in despair.

"After all, God is in charge. Knowing that, I could never feel hopeless. It's like wading through deep sand and finally feeling the rock beneath it."

■

One of the questions nonChristians like to ask is, "What difference does being a Christian make?" When we look at the lives of people like Virginia, that difference is clear: it's the difference between being defeated and being victorious. Paul described the difference this way:

We are hard pressed on every side, but not crushed. We all feel hard pressed now and then—pressured by obligations, burdened by concerns, pushed to our limits by the day-to-day demands on us. And yet God sustains us. We can greet each day as a new start, knowing that we may falter, but that God will not fail us.

We are perplexed, but not in despair. Life can be baffling. We all ask from time to time why tragedy befalls good people (ourselves included); why evil seems to triumph over good; why there is so much inhumanity, greed, injustice, and suffering in the world. We are indeed perplexed. Yet when we trust in God's infinite wisdom and His eternal perspective instead of our own limited understanding, our perplexity does not turn into despair.

We are persecuted, but not abandoned. Taking a stand for Christian principles in a worldly setting can be lonely. Being the employee who refuses to cheat on expenses or take advantage of an employer or engage in office flirtations makes us different—not a part of the group. Being criticized or ridiculed for our beliefs can hurt. We may feel isolated and out of place, but we are never alone, never abandoned.

We are struck down, but not destroyed. When Virginia learned of her husband's illness, she must have felt struck down. When a job layoff comes, or a loved one dies, or a relationship ends, the pain can be like a physical blow. But God promises us the courage to keep on going, to recover from life's blows with greater strength than before—battered and bruised maybe, but not destroyed.

Virginia's friends saw that, when life's trials piled up on her, she demonstrated courage and faith and retained her concern for the needs of others. Each of us, in our darkest times, our most trying days, has the opportunity to witness for Christ in this way. Those around us look to see how we handle the real tests of faith. It's another chance to demonstrate that being a Christian does make a difference.

PRAYER

God, I feel reassured to know that no matter what trials life brings me, You are always there. I recommit myself to trusting You more fully. Help me to be an example for You, to let others see how You make victory possible when life's circumstances threaten to defeat me. Amen.

THIRTY

This Year's Newest Model

*She is clothed with strength and dignity;
she can laugh at the days to come. She speaks
with wisdom, and faithful instruction
is on her tongue.*

Proverbs 31:25-26

    distinguish between the world's model and God's model for working women;

    redefine our priorities.

Wendy is on vacation from her job as assistant manager of a retail store. The kids are at school, she's finished the laundry, and she's even cleaned out the freezer in the basement—a job that she's been dreading for months. Now she's going to treat herself to some real vacation-type leisure: watch reruns of her favorite old sitcoms on television and eat a bowl of butter pecan ice cream. This is the life!

Naturally, every ten minutes the sitcoms are interrupted for commercials. In the first one, a smartly dressed businesswoman breezes into her son's second-grade birthday party with a whole tray of delightfully decorated cupcakes. The teacher and the other mothers ooh and ahh and say, "How do you do it? Your job, the kids — and still find time to bake!" Naturally, she tells them her secret is Quick 'n' Gooey cupcake mix. As the commercial ends, the woman's son hugs her and says, "You're such a good mom!"

In the next commercial, about a dozen neighborhood children are playing in one woman's yard, and she's serving them soft drinks and sandwiches and smiling all the while.

The third commercial to interrupt Wendy's television viewing shows a woman hostessing a dinner party. She's wearing a long silky dress and dishing up something that looks as if it came directly from a gourmet restaurant. Her husband is beaming with pride as the guests marvel and say, "I just don't know how she does it!"

For some reason, Wendy finds that her sitcom just doesn't seem very funny today. In fact, she feels kind of depressed. She wants, more than anything, to be a good wife and mother and a conscientious employee. Seeing the women in those television commercials makes her wonder if she's doing a very good job at anything. She doesn't bake fancy cupcakes or entertain the whole neighborhood's kids or orchestrate dazzling social occasions. She doesn't dress like a magazine cover, and her house is a little dusty. She feels a creeping sense of self-doubt. Is she a dismal failure? Is every other working woman so much better at everything than she is?

■

Today's working woman is the target of an unrelenting media blitz designed to tell us how we ought to look, act, dress, think, and feel. Because the media bombard us so constantly, it's easy for us to start to believe in the models and standards they set.

But what is God's model of the ideal working woman? What kind of wives, mothers, friends, and employees does He want us to be?

To find the answer, let's look at the working women's role model, that inspiring and exciting woman we meet in Proverbs 31. What kind of woman is she?

She is practical. She thinks before she acts. The Bible tells us she "considers" a purchase before she makes it (verse 16). She exercises good judgment in business matters; as the Bible puts it, she "sees that her trading is profitable" (verse 18). She plans ahead; she can "laugh at the days to come" (verse 25) because she has prepared for them.

She is generous. Even though her days are busy from dawn to dusk and she's careful about money, she still finds the time and the resources to "open her arms to the poor and extend her hands to the needy" (verse 20).

She speaks wisely. She isn't interested in gossiping or being a busybody. When she says something, it's wise and instructive (verse 26). She uses her words to build up others.

She brings good into the lives of others. She feels a sense of responsibility for her family, her servants, and the needy people of her community. She cares about their needs and desires. Her husband "has full confidence in her" (verse 11); and she "brings him good" in the eyes of others (verse 12); her children praise her (verse 28); all those who know her respect her (verse 31). She inspires them all.

She manages herself well. She's able to juggle her many responsibilities—managing her businesses, running her home, caring for her family—and yet, she still finds time to be compassionate, supportive, and spiritually rich. She schedules her time carefully so that she has time to do the things that are important. She doesn't waste time by "eating the bread of idleness" (verse 27), nor does she live in a constant state of frustrated overcommitment. She uses her time in a way that reflects her true priorities.

The Bible's model of a working woman

isn't concerned with proving that she's the best mother on the block or with meeting the world's expectations about how she ought to look or think or believe. This woman's priorities are clear: first and foremost, she fears the Lord; second, she looks to the needs of her family; third, she exercises her responsibilities to the larger human community, from the people in her household to the poor and the needy outside her doors.

Maybe if we were equally clear about our priorities, we could more easily fulfill our many roles as working women.

PRAYER

Lord, help me to be a Proverbs 31 woman. Help me to clarify my own priorities, so that I'm not always at the mercy of what the world thinks I ought to do and be. I want to bring good into the lives of others; I want to be practical, generous, wise, and efficient. Thank You for this wonderful role model from Your Word. Amen.

THIRTY-ONE

If You Please

*Although he was a son, he learned obedience
from what he suffered and, once made perfect,
he became the source of eternal salvation
for all who obey him.*

Hebrews 5:8-9

LET'S SLOW DOWN TODAY TO...

ה *reassure ourselves of our God-given worth;*

ה *reevaluate the expectations others have of us;*

ה *practice accepting unconditional love.*

A few months ago I was a speaker at a Christian women's conference out of town. I was flattered and excited about being asked to speak; but as I looked ahead to the trip, I worried and worried about what to wear for the conference. A voice in my head kept asking me, "How will these women expect me to look? What kind of clothes will make them respond most positively to me?" In other words, I wanted to make a good impression.

One day shortly before the conference, I was browsing in a local shopping mall, just hoping some perfect outfit would jump off the rack at me. As I rummaged through the racks of clothes, I was suddenly struck by the silliness of my worries about what to wear. My purpose in going to the conference was to bring a message of encouragement and inspiration to the women attending—not to give them the latest fashion tips! I had lost my focus on that goal and had become consumed with conforming to my listeners' expectations.

Now I certainly don't think there's anything wrong with wanting to please others. In fact, in a world obsessed with self-centeredness, the Bible calls us to genuine concern for the interests of others (Philippians 2:4). There's a danger, though, in striving too hard to please others. We may begin to measure our own inherent worth only by how well we meet others' expectations.

All of us feel a certain amount of pressure to conform to the standards and expectations of whatever group or groups are most important to us—our bosses and coworkers, our families, our friends, our fellow church members. That's natural. The apostle Paul even says he went out of his way to become "all things to all men" (1 Corinthians 9:22)—just as you and I often find ourselves trying to be everything to everybody.

Paul's goal in doing so, however, was not to please them and win their approval, but to "win as many as possible" for Christ

(1 Corinthians 9:19). We as women often wear ourselves out trying to be everything to everybody, not in order to win souls for Christ, but so that we will feel loved and needed. When our sense of self-worth runs low, we try to shore it up by seeking love and approval from others.

Perhaps what we need to learn is how to rest in the assurance that we are valuable in God's sight. Then we can attend to the needs of others out of genuine love and compassion, not out of our need to feel valuable.

Another pitfall of seeking to please others above all else is that it may tempt us to adopt human values instead of godly ones as the basis for our decision-making. We may suddenly be willing to compromise our values in order to please someone else: the boss who wants us to lie about where he was that afternoon when *his* boss came looking for him; the boyfriend or husband who cares more about our outward appearance than our inner beauty; the friend who asks if we could steal some office supplies from our workplace so that she can use them in her home business.

A third danger of the overly eager-to-please mindset is that we may begin to believe God — as well as people — will love us only if we measure up to His expectations.

One day when I went to lunch with my friend Peggy, I found myself doing an unusual amount of griping and moaning about my job and saying assorted unpleasant, negative things about work, people, and life in general. Finally, I said, "Just listen to how I sound! You must think I'm a terrible person to say things like this."

Peggy smiled her world-class smile and said, "Don't you know that your friends love you — even if you say terrible things; even on your worst days? That's why they're your friends — because they love you."

Peggy's friendship isn't based on how I act on any given day; she loves me for who I am. None of us is consistent enough in our behavior to count on pleasing our friends all the time. Sure, there are people who want to be our friends as long as we meet their needs and expectations; but those relationships, fortunately, don't usually last very long.

God's love is the model for the unconditional love that we as Christians aspire to. We can't measure up to His standards any more than we can always measure up to our friends' standards. But He loves us anyway. Yes, we desire to please Him; and, yes, His standards are what we strive for. But perfection is not a prerequisite of His love.

Jesus Christ's sacrificial death has already made us perfect in God's sight.

PRAYER

God, I thank You that You love me in spite of my shortcomings – because there are so many. Teach me to love others in the same way. Help me learn to accept unconditional love – from You and from others – with gratitude and grace. Amen.

THIRTY-TWO

Work, Work, Work

*Then they asked him, "What must we do to do
the works God requires?"
Jesus answered, "The work of God is this:
to believe in the one he has sent."*

John 6:28-29

LET'S SLOW DOWN TODAY TO...

❧ *reflect on God's plan for our lives and the role of work in it;*

❧ *think about what it means to do God's work.*

My friend John is a very successful novelist. He and I have often commiserated on the pitfalls and perils of being a writer. Here is one of his "war stories" that I enjoy the most:

John was making casual conversation with a man to whom he was just introduced.

"What kind of work do you do?" the man asked him.

"I'm a writer," John replied.

"Oh," the man responded. "And do you have a *real* job, too?"

■

John and I have laughed about this story many times. We have both learned, over the years, that most people don't view writing as a *real* job. To us, as we deal from day to day with the drudgery, frustration, isolation, and total exasperation that writing for a living brings, writing is indeed a *real* job, even though to many others it doesn't seem like one. That's okay. No one ever said it would be glamorous!

Just as many people fail to understand the nature of writing as work, many of us may be equally unclear about the nature of God's work. As Christians, we know we are called to do God's work, but what is it? When we have a job outside the home, a household to run, relationships to maintain, church and community responsibilities, and our own physical and emotional well-being to preserve, where do we squeeze in time to do God's work—assuming, of course, that we can figure out what it is?

My friend Dawn is a missionary with an international evangelistic organization. She travels to Spanish-speaking countries in Central and South America and spreads the gospel through Bible studies, small-group meetings, and personal evangelism. No one would question whether she is doing God's work.

What about you and me? In my job as public relations manager for a health care agency (which is my *real* job in addition to writing), am I doing God's work; or do I only do His work when I'm writing Christian books? What about Renee, who is a clerk in a discount store? Is she doing God's work? What about Kim, who is a lawyer? Or Kathy, who is a sculptor? Or Carolyn, who is a homemaker? Or what about you?

As young people, we are often led to feel that only missionaries, pastors, and others in full-time Christian service are doing God's work. Many of us have struggled and tormented ourselves with the question of what work God would have us do for Him.

A few years ago, I came across the Scripture quoted at the beginning of this chapter. Suddenly it was all much clearer to me. Our work is simply being Christians: believing in the saving work of God through Christ and living the life to which we are called. That's our full-time job. It supersedes all other work we do. It pervades every hour of our days and nights. It is our first and foremost employment. Everything else we do in our day-to-day lives—on the job, at home, in our leisure-time activities—is simply an aspect of that employment.

In other words, the type of earthly job we have isn't what determines whether we are doing God's work. We are doing God's work if we are committed to living by His principles as exemplified in Christ. Whether we are taco makers or medical supply salespersons or corporate executives doesn't change our fundamental occupation, which is being Christians.

I was discussing this with Dawn, my missionary friend, just recently. I told her that I thought many people were intimidated when they met missionaries face-to-face. Being in the presence of a missionary makes the rest of us feel guilty that we haven't been willing to make the same sacrifices they have, that is, to do God's work on a full-time basis. That feeling stems from our lack of understanding about what God's work really is.

"God's work would never get done if everyone was in full-time missions work," Dawn said to me. She went on to discuss the fact that God needs people everywhere, working for Him and living for Him as they go about their daily lives in offices, schools, stores, neighborhoods, factories, restaurants — everywhere.

You and I don't need to go looking for new jobs in order to go about God's work. We are called to His harvest field; to bear witness for Him in an angry, hateful, hurting world. We do His work every day when we represent Him in our work setting, whatever that might be.

Now that's a *real* job!

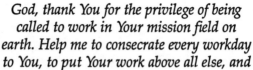

PRAYER

God, thank You for the privilege of being called to work in Your mission field on earth. Help me to consecrate every workday to You, to put Your work above all else, and to be a clear witness for You to those with whom I work. May I be on the job for You every moment of every day. Amen.